MARY CELESTE
A CENTENARY RECORD

Also by Macdonald Hastings

The 'Mr Cork' Books
CORK ON THE WATER
CORK IN BOTTLE
CORK AND THE SERPENT
CORK IN THE DOGHOUSE
CORK ON THE TELLY

Historical Novel
A GLIMPSE OF ARCADIA

A Personal History
JESUIT CHILD

War Reminiscence
PASSED AS CENSORED

Anthology
MACDONALD HASTINGS' COUNTRY BOOK

Text Books
CHURCHILL ON GAME SHOOTING
HOW TO SHOOT STRAIGHT
ENGLISH SPORTING GUNS

Biography
THE OTHER MR CHURCHILL

For Boys
EAGLE SPECIAL INVESTIGATOR
ADVENTURE CALLING
THE SEARCH FOR THE LITTLE YELLOW MEN
MEN OF GLORY
MORE MEN OF GLORY

For Little Children
SYDNEY SPARROW

For Television
CALL THE GUN EXPERT (A SERIES)
RIVERBEAT (TWO SERIES)
VOYAGE INTO ENGLAND (A SERIES)
IN DEEPEST BRITAIN (A SERIES)
THE HATED SOCIETY : THE JESUITS

MARY CELESTE: Latitude 38° 20' N, Longitude
70° 15' W on December 4, 1872 (December 5 seatime).
An artist's reconstruction of the appearance of the
derelict brig when she was first sighted by the crew of
the *Dei Gratia*

John Wosley

MARY CELESTE

A CENTENARY RECORD

Macdonald Hastings

'History is a distillation of rumour.'
Th. Carlyle

MICHAEL JOSEPH   LONDON

First published in Great Britain in 1972 by Michael Joseph Ltd
52 Bedford Square, London, W.C.1

© 1972 by Macdonald Hastings

7181 1024 2

Set and printed in Great Britain by
Tonbridge Printers Ltd, Peach Hall Works, Tonbridge, Kent
in Janson eleven on thirteen point on paper supplied by
P. F. Bingham Ltd, and bound by James Burn
at Esher, Surrey

To
SUSAN HARRIET SELINA HASTINGS
– No mystery she –
with her father's love

CONTENTS

ILLUSTRATIONS

Frontispiece

Mary Celeste, a derelict in the Atlantic, on December 4, 1872. A watercolour by John Worsley

Between pages 80–81

Captain Benjamin Spooner Briggs, master of the *Mary Celeste*

Mrs. Briggs, the master's wife, with her son, Arthur Stanley, who was left behind in New England

Albert Richardson, first mate of the *Mary Celeste*

Sophia Matilda Briggs, the two-year-old daughter of the master, who was lost with them at sea

Captain David Reed Morehouse, master of the *Dei Gratia*

Oliver Deveau, first mate of the *Dei Gratia*

'Abel Fosdyke's' story, as it was illustrated in the *Strand Magazine*

The Rock of Gibraltar as in the middle of the nineteenth century

The publisher's announcement of Keating's book, *The Great Mary Celeste Hoax*

The 'bloodstained' sword which played such a part in the story

The Briggs melodeon, still preserved by a descendant of the family in New England

1. THE MAKING OF A LEGEND

Man-made things that move, and especially handmade things, have a life of their own. There are individual traits in motor cars, guns, even the flow of a ballpoint pen, which are essentially extensions of ourselves. Less than life, they have a strange adequacy. It is particularly true of sailing ships, ruled by wind and tide. This is about the ship found abandoned in latitude 38° 20′ N, longitude 17° 15′ W on December 4, 1872 (December 5, seatime) which prompts the thought more remarkably than any of the stories of the sea. It is of the little brig which sailed, perhaps ten days, without a living soul aboard her.

The tall stories which have been told about the *Mary Celeste* for a hundred years after she was found a derelict between the Azores and the coast of Portugal have been tall as her masts. Wild whispers were fanned by her flapping sails in the first hours when she made a landfall in Gibraltar in December, 1872. Hints of dark doings were ascribed to every one of her ropes, spars and timbers. If she had vanished without trace, with her master and crew, the world would never have heard of her, nor cared. But she sailed on, alone. The silent witness of what really happened, she has stirred men's imagination, cupidity and invention ever since.

I have no new wonder to advance except to tell how *Mary Celeste*, a sort of wanton, has seduced men's minds. Only one had any good out of her. He made the beginnings of his name with an anonymous short story in the *Cornhill Magazine* in which he got her name wrong. He called her 'Marie Celeste' and the mistake has stuck.

Arthur Conan Doyle was one who never had any intimacy with her. But the great storyteller made her reputation.

She was a brig, a half-brig, sometimes called a hermaphrodite brig, with two masts. The foremast was square-rigged and the mainmast fore-and-aft, or schooner rigged. She had what is called a billet head and a square stern and, at her launching, only one deck. Her statistics were: length, 99.3 feet, breadth 25.5 feet, depth 11.7 feet. Her gross tonnage was 198.42.

Her keel was laid in Nova Scotia in 1860. She was the maiden venture of a consortium of pioneers on Spencer's Island. In a clearing in the virgin forest they built her out of the stands of big timber all about. She was birch, beech and maple up to the light load line, then spruce to the rails, with pine to finish the cabins. On her foundation blocks she was a trim little thing, a happy reward for the enterprise of hardy men who had hewed her with their axes out of the Canadian wilderness. When they launched her into the Atlantic in 1861, they named her *Amazon*, wishing God's blessing on all who sailed in her.

How the devil got into her timbers, fathered by such God-fearing worthy men, is a riddle. As well ask what turns the daughter of a respectable family into a whore. At the start of her dance on the sea she was certainly disappointed in first love. On her maiden voyage her master, a young Scot named Robert McLellan, was taken ill at Quaco, near St John, N.B. He sailed her home to die a few days later in her home port.

For the next six years she sailed from North American ports in industrious anonymity, carrying cargoes between England, the West Indies and the Mediterranean. In 1867, she had the shock which changed her character. At Cow Bay, Cape Breton, where she had gone to load coal for New York, she went ashore in a gale. She was sold to the best buyer.

In the sad way of orphans she passed through various

owners until, at last, she became the property of an American syndicate who repaired her. Her name was changed to *Mary Celeste*. The new owners were 'James H. Winchester, twelve twenty-fourths; Sylvester Goodwin, two twenty-fourths; Daniel T. Sampson, two twenty-fourths; Benjamin S. Briggs of Marion, State of Maine, eight twenty-fourths.' She was given two decks instead of one as before. Her length was increased to 103 feet, her breadth to 25.7 feet. Her total tonnage was now 282.28. Her topsail was divided, for the sake of easier handling, into an upper and lower sail. Her new master, Benjamin Briggs, was delighted with her. 'Our vessel is in beautiful trim' he wrote to his mother before he sailed on his fateful voyage. 'I hope we shall have a fine passage; but as I have never been in her before can't say how she'll sail.'

In the event she sailed more mysteriously than any ship has sailed. Nobody knows, nor ever will, what happened aboard her. Seamen who regard ships as people, creatures which will answer for one helmsman and behave like mules for another, also believe that ships have hearts, either for the good or for the bad.

Maybe, *Mary Celeste* broke her own heart when her first master died, or when she ran ashore at Cow Bay. Maybe she enjoyed being a puzzling bitch when they brought her into Gibraltar with none of her company left to tell the tale. Twenty-five years after, when she was a raddled hag, her then crew wrecked her, in hope of insurance money, on a reef of the Rochelais, near Mirgeone, Haiti. They, too, came to sticky ends.

It is significant that not even the bare details of *Mary Celeste*'s birth, life and death – overwhelming as the evidence seems to be – have been universally accepted. Truth, there is no ultimate truth, exists only in what you believe. The evidence of any eye witness, however honestly given, is suspect. The interpretation of events, with the best will in the world, is invariably and inevitably biased. The story of *Mary Celeste* is a classic not of what maybe happened but of what people for so many reasons for so many years have chosen to suppose did happen.

While I think that I guess a solution, I am fascinated by men who have held different opinions to my own. Not the least of them the officials of the Vice Admiralty Court of Gibraltar who arrested *Mary Celeste* when she was brought in by the crew of the British brig, *Dei Gratia*. They lived in the time it happened, not ours.

It is history that the Vice Admiralty Court, sitting in enquiry on the salvage claim from December 17, 1872 to March 5, 1873, described the brig as 'the ship or vessel supposed to be called *Mary Celeste*'. Subsequently, even the identity of the ship's company has been challenged. It is proper to emphasise that, from the time the derelict was brought into Gibraltar, officialdom was convinced that the crew of the *Dei Gratia* were all liars.

In this account I have given my imagination just a little sail but only enough, as I believe, to evoke the mood at the time. I have written what seems to be true, however much the story has been confused by contemporary and latter day writers.

You are the judge of the affair.

2. CONFUSION WORSE CONFOUNDED

I have in my keeping a yellowing book of press clippings assembled over a period of fifty years by a sailing ship's master named T. E. Elwell. He lent it to me in the early fifties when he was in retirement in the Isle of Man. Subsequently, when I tried to return the book to him, the package came back marked 'gone away'. He himself had indeed gone away; but the mystery, out of which he had made a hobby for almost half a lifetime, has the quality of immortality.

He sent me his cuttings' book because I had been guilty of an article in the boys' magazine *Eagle* in which I had been fooled into accepting one of the fictional versions of the fate of *Mary Celeste*. Captain Elwell, lacking latter knowledge, had earlier been misled himself. In his book he pasted an article of his own, which had appeared in *Chambers' Journal* in the twenties, which is manifestly misinformed. But so much nonsense has been written that, while I intend to make what amends I can here, it is salutory to start with a sampling of the legends which have infected the story of the brig from the time when she was brought into Gibraltar by her salvors and ever after.

So much hearsay has stuck, so much fiction has come to be accepted as fact, that it is important to emphasise that there is not much more than a word or two of truth in the chapter which follows. Here are simply examples, from Captain Elwell's scrap book, of the extent of human credulity. The mystery of *Mary Celeste* is not the less for it but, rather, more exciting.

'A minute examination of the vessel revealed a truly

15

extraordinary and astounding state of affairs. There was not a single boat missing. They were all in their proper places slung on the davits and stowed on deck in the usual manner. Further than that, not a rope or stay, not a sail or spar, was injured. Everything, from truck to keel, was as sound as the day the vessel had sailed. More astonishingly still, the captain's watch was ticking on a nail above his berth, and on the cabin's table was found the remains of a half-consumed dinner, apparently as fresh as when it came from the cook's galley.' (*J. L Hornibrook, Oct. 1, 1904.*)

'The forecastle was silent and deserted. The vessel had been abandoned precipitately for no apparent reason. The brig's boats, two, stood firm in their chocks on the roof of the deckhouse. . . . The galley range, although raked out, was still hot. A cat was sleeping peacefully on the locker. On a table in the after-cabin a meal was laid. The viands were cold, but three cups of tea which stood by the plates were still luke-warm.' (*Lee Kaye, July, 1926.*)

'I see the mate standing his trick at the wheel, oblivious of the steady removal of the fore hatches under cover of the forward house. I see a barrel broached, two men filling a couple of buckets, and replacing the hatches and tarpaulin. They begin to drink, grow quarrelsome, and are soon at each other's throats. There comes a cry of horror, for one has loosened his grip, and his victim sinks lifeless to the deck. The mate releases the wheel and rushes forward, to be met with a blow on the head with a belaying-pin. . . . So two bodies are tumbled over the side, and the murderer turns again to the bucket. He exults, sings, raves, fights imaginary enemies, and while crouching on the topgallant bulwarks, shaking his fists at the screaming gulls, he leans too far, slips, and is the last of the *Mary Celeste*'s crew to die.' (*T. E. Elwell, circa early thirties.*)

'The man stationed at the wheel is alone on deck. All the others have gone below to their midday meal. Suddenly a huge octopus rises from the deep, and rearing one of its terrible arms aloft encircles the helmsman. His yells bring every soul on board rushing on deck. One by one they are caught by the waving, wriggling arms and swept overboard. Then, freighted with its living load, the monster slowly sinks into the deep again, leaving no traces of its attack.' (*J. L. Hornibrook, 1904.*)

'Sir, . . . I happen to know some of the people connected with the *Mary Celeste* . . . I happen to know that she had two good boats and that they were on board when the *Dei Gratia* picked her up . . . Henry Bilson, who figures as the 'missing mate', was not on board the *Mary Celeste* that last voyage. I was well acquainted with Bilson, who was my father's bosom chum, for I lived in New York from sixty-seven to ninety; and I corresponded with him from England till ninety-three, when he died. The fact was that the *Mary Celeste* left New York when the place was upside down through the authorities acting against the crimps. The latter had only to wag a finger and a whole crew would walk off the ship. The consequence was no one knew who was on a ship for certain when she sailed.' (*A letter from William Adams to John O'London's Weekly, 1927.*)

'John Pemberton, who sailed on the famous voyage of the *Marie Celeste*, has recently died. Before his death he gave permission for the true facts to be revealed, putting an end to one of the most romantic legends of the sea.' (*Roland Wild, in The People, 1939.*)

'I SOLVE THE MYSTERY OF THE MARIE CELESTE' (*Commander Campbell of the B.B.C.'s Brains Trust, in the Sunday Dispatch, 1942*).

The stories have multiplied over the years. The wild

inventions which have stormed into the tale are revelations of what imaginative people enjoyed imagining.

Never mind dear old salts like Commander Campbell who began his tall tale, characteristically: 'One night we were lying alongside the wharf at Wooloomooloo, Sydney Harbour. Some of us were yarning on the fo'csle head when a youngster mentioned the case of the *Marie Celeste*. He related the tale as he had heard it. An old bos'n named Pike listened intently. And, when the man had finished he looked him in the face and said: "As a sailor, do you really believe all that junk?" "Well," answered the man, "it's one solution, isn't it?" "Not the right one by a long chalk," I butted in. "What do you know about it then, Pike?"'

In his article Commander Campbell then repeated, with a few variations of names and details, lies which had been perpetrated by somebody else. Campbell, a professional romancer, knew nothing of *Mary Celeste*, and repeated the fantasy of a Liverpool Irishman, himself a dreamer of dreams, who knew nothing of the matter either.

In attempting a definitive history, I have told the facts, so far as they can be extracted from the records. I have had fun dramatising the entertainment of the more notorious fictions.

3. THE *DEI GRATIA*'S STORY

A small sailing ship is swagging aimlessly in a squally sea. She yaws and falls off, her sails panting as she pitches in and out of the wind. Her rig is square on the foremast, for and aft on the main. Only her lower tops'l jib and foretop stays'l are set. The other sails are torn to rags, or furled. The day is grey and, in the uneasy sea, she could be a mere shadow, the sort of ship that is imagined rather than real.

A rowboat's eye view of the square stern reveals her name painted fair on the woodwork: 'MARY CELESTE, NEW YORK'. An untended ship's wheel, in a greaseless brass bearing, spins with a monotonous groaning, first one way, then the other. Water is gulping out of the open door of the galley in the forward deckhouse every time her helm swings as she pitches into the wind. Ends of running rigging sweep her deck. Her main stays'l lies draped over the galley chimney. She presents a picture of wet desolation.

A voice hails her through a speaking trumpet 'Brig, ahoy! Brig, ahoy.' The ship drives unhearingly on her drunken course. The hail, repeated several times, draws nearer. Nothing moves on deck except a water cask which has burst away from the chocks linking it with others in the front of the aft deck housing. Nothing else shifts except a fore hatch lying beside the open hold. The arms of the ship's pumps, pivoted on iron posts fore of the main-mast, make a lazy semaphore. A silent comment is a displaced binnacle, housing a broken compass.

The head of a heavily bearded man raises over the chain plates in the bow. He looks about him anxiously. He has no guess that, a month later, he will be standing with his hands resting on the rails, not of a sailing ship but a witness box, accounting for what he found. A Canadian, he was to be cross-examined in the Gibraltar court by an officious Irishman who disbelieved everything he told.

'Mr Deveau, you are the chief mate of the British vessel, *Dei Gratia*.'

'Yes, I am.'

'And you say that, when you climbed aboard the American vessel, *Mary Celeste*, now lying in Gibraltar Harbour, she was sailing herself with not a living soul aboard her, six hundred miles out in the Atlantic. That sounds an improbable tale.'

'That's how it was.'

'Would you be good enough to tell the Court what you would have us believe happened?'

'On the fifth of December, seatime, during my watch below, the captain called and said that there was a strange sail on the windward bow apparently in distress, and requiring assistance.'

Oliver Deveau parrotted his evidence, to the annoyance of the court, like a policeman.

'I came on deck and saw a vessel through the glass. She appeared about four or five miles off. The master proposed to speak the vessel in order to render assistance if necessary, and to haul wind for that purpose which we did. By dead reckoning of our own ship, we were 38° 20′ North latitude, 17°....'

'Yes, yes, Mr Deveau. All that has already been stated. When you went aboard the *Mary Celeste* you were accompanied by another man.'

'John Wright, second mate.'

'The court of enquiry, Mr Deveau, will call him later for corroboration of your evidence. Meanwhile, I am sure that His Lordship would prefer to have your own story in your own words.'

'Well, whether you believe or not, it was like this:

The sea was running high but, leaving a seaman to watch our ship's boat, John Wright and me got aboard by the chains.'

The first mate of the *Dei Gratia* little knew that it was to be a moment of history when he came over her side, and dropped on to the deck of *Mary Celeste*. He was followed by the younger man, John Wright. The two of them stared at the ship, and each other, in amazement. Both were barefooted. Both were dressed in the miscellaneous clothing of all merchant seamen of the time. Both spoke with Canadian accents. Hollering through cupped hands, 'Anyone aboard ' they waited half-hopefully for a reply. The only comment came from the sea, washing the decks of the deserted ship.

Simple men as they were they must have been nervous.

'Ship's boat gone. Look, a rail lifted on the portside.'

'Best watch our own boat. I'll shout the hand to stand by until we come off.'

'Looks as if she has shipped a lot of sea.'

'Leaking badly, I guess. Let's sound the pumps.'

'Box off. Sounding rod gone.'

'They must have been sounding when they abandoned her.'

It is easy, in afterthought, to believe that two rough seamen were undismayed. The Vice Admiralty Court of Gibraltar clearly thought that they were associated in a conspiracy. Even if they were, it calls for uncommon courage to board a deserted ship in the wilderness of the Atlantic. Deveau, the first mate, showed the will to command.

'See if you can find the rod, or a bit of weighted line to drop down. I'm going below.'

Apprehensively, the second mate hesitated.

'It couldn't be Yellow Jack, could it?'

'I'm going below.'

Deveau, he hadn't got to go far in a ship little more

than a hundred feet overall, padded along the side of the deckhousing to the poop, leaving Wright to search the deck. The deckhouse had windows, but they were battened up. A skylight was open. On the poop, Deveau glanced at the broken binnacle. Then, with a hook of his bare foot, he threw back a sliding door, already half-open, at the fore-end of the deckhouse. With a duck of his head he dropped down the companionway.

Inside the cabin, such light as there was came through the skylight. Deveau felt his way with the haste of a burglar. At the foot of the companionway a swinging door showed the entrance to the chief mate's cabin. To the right he had a glimpse of the pantry. The little saloon, finished in pine, was furnished with little more than tables and benches, and a sideboard. Abaft the saloon, with an entrance on the left, was the captain's cabin.

Deveau struck a match for closer inspection. On the saloon table, he found the Log Slate, chalked with an entry for November 25. He noticed a clock, without hands, on the saloon wall. In the captain's cabin he discovered a melodeon, with a piece of sheet music on it, against the partition dividing the cabin from the saloon. There was a sewing machine on a writing desk. There were bits of women's clothing, and a child's toys. He found trinkets and money. He felt a double bed, soaked with seawater, in which the pillow was impressed with a child's head. Under the bed he pulled out a sort of cutlass. Half-drawing it from the scabbard, he returned it disinterestedly to its place. He found bags of clothes stowed under the berth.

In the darkness of the mate's cabin he broke the glass and the battening used to close it against the weather with a blow of a hammer from a box of carpenter's tools. He studied a log book on the table, and a chart pinned over the bunk.

He emerged into the gloomy daylight on deck.

'Nobody aboard.'

John Wright welcomed him with a relief of his own.

'No sounding rod, but I found a bit of line with a bolt on the end. They must have used that. Three and half feet of water, that's all. A couple of hours work, and we can pump her dry.'

The twin pumps of the *Mary Celeste* were of the simplest kind. An iron post was bolted to the deck. Pivoted at the top was a five foot T-piece with T-pieces at each of its ends to form handles. Without comment, Deveau worked the pumps. He satisfied himself, looking over the side, that water was gushing sweetly from the outlet ducts.

'No one would have abandoned her with that little water, and the pumps working.'

Deveau nodded his agreement.

'Check the stores in the lazarette. I'll go forward, you aft.'

In the galley, swimming up to the sill below the door in seawater, Deveau entered the crew's quarters. Washing was hanging on the line. The men's oilskins, boots, pipes and razors and three seamen's chests were the way they had left them. On deck again, Wright was enthusiastic.

'Six months stores, and water. A cargo of alcohol in the hold.'

Deveau looked thoughtfully about him.

'Standing rigging sound. Most of the running rigging carried away.'

'We could fix it in a couple of days. If we put her to rights, we could sail the world in her.'

'You're right, we could.'

Neither of them, with the third hand bobbing in the rowboat in the bow, guessed what was in store for them. Captain Morehouse, of their own brig, watched what went on through his glass, with his speaking trumpet on the deck at his side. He was a middle-aged man with a beard split at the centre like an agreeable goat. Assessing the state of *Mary Celeste*, heaving and falling in the wind, he can scarcely have been less than hopeful that he had a valuable prize. He waited, one supposes eagerly, as his men pulled back from the deserted ship.

'She's staunch and sound, sir.'

'Abandoned?'

'The last entry on the Log Slate is November 25. She had made the Island of St Mary's bearing East-South-East.'

The captain was puzzled. Reaching for a chart he calculated her position with a pair of dividers.

'Sure that you're right?'

'Yes, sir.'

'Ship's boat gone?'

'She only had one by the look of it, which was on chocks on the main hatch. There's a spar lashed across the stern davits, so no boat's been there.'

If they abandoned her on November 25, she's been sailing on her own for nine days or more. According to my reckoning she is 500 to 750 miles east and northwards of her last position.'

'Changing course all the time.'

'An unmanned ship. Sounds impossible.'

Deveau and Wright waited impetuously for their turn to speak.

'We could put her to rights in a few days' work.'

'We could sail the world in her.'

'The binnacle's stove in and the chronometer, sextant and navigation book seems to be missing.'

'She's got a full cargo of crude alcohol.'

Morehouse played the captain's part.

'I know what you're thinking. But our crew, Deveau, is seven. Six hundred miles of the Atlantic, in mid-winter, lie between us and Gibraltar. I owe it to you, and the owners, to bring my own ship safely into port.'

'Four could handle the *Die Gratia*. Three could bring in the *Mary Celeste*.'

Deveau was insistent.

'I have commanded a brig before.'

Morehouse smiled.

'Yes, we could all do with the salvage money.'

As the captain paced his deck, Deveau and Wright waited eagerly for his decision. They can hardly have expected from a penniless commander that it would be other than it was.

'Very well, if the whole crew agrees, I am willing.'

'They will, sir.'

'I know. I'll give you two men, Deveau, the ship's small boat, a barometer, compass and watch and any food prepared in the galley. I don't know what the owners are going to say but I'll chance it. If you can bring her in, we are in luck.'

Luck has seldom been such a double-faced coin. If they won the toss on the sea, they thought that they could not fail in a claim for valuable salvage. Against all the odds they won over the sulky Atlantic only to find, when they made Gibraltar, that they were met by faceless officials who, in unconscionable legal enquiry, seemed to insist: 'Heads I win, tails you lose.'

It was a brave gamble when they won the first flick, chancing two ships in mid-winter with a quarter as many hands on them as sails. They were in an ocean, seven hundred miles from a safe anchorage, which can treat an eighty thousand ton liner, engined with all the power of contemporary technology, served by hundreds of men, as disrespectfully as a match box. They sailed, eight men, in two wooden ships, their joint displacement not much more than five hundred tons. One of them was a saggy derelict with her running rigging a cat's cradle, her binnacle unhoused, her sails in rags.

All Captain Morehouse could spare from his own brig was a small boat, a very small boat, a barometer, compass and watch. The chief mate took with him his own nautical instruments and such rough food as the steward of the

Die Gratia had prepared. He borrowed two able seamen, Augustus Anderson and Charles Lund. The second mate, John Wright, who had boarded with him the first time, stayed behind on the *Dei Gratia* to mate her on her own run to Gibraltar. The other hand, John Johnson, who rowed the boat when they discovered the derelict, stayed on the *Dei Gratia*, too. In spite of his name, he was of Russian origin, and he had only a few words of English.

I don't know what parting Captain Morehouse and Oliver Deveau made. It was probably nautically brief. But it appears that they agreed, so far as they could, to keep each other in sight and, if possible, in speaking distance. They both recognised the risk that they were taking in getting the undermanned ships into port. In trouble the hope was that, if they lost one of the two, they could get together again to save the other.

Oliver Deveau, with less than overnight baggage, dropped over the side into the dinghy to keep his appointment with destiny. His two seamen tumbled after him. To most people the swell of the Atlantic, as they oared the distance, even if it was only a few hundred yards, would have been the adventure of a lifetime. In the trough of the uneasy swell they can scarcely have sighted their own ship, or the derelict they were going to. Hanging on to their precious navigational aids and their provisions, the hungry sea hunted them up to their gunwails.

Deveau had made his judgment, after a mere half-an-hour aboard, that he could get *Mary Celeste* to port. He would have been less than human if, with only two hands, he was confident that he could pump her out, and put her to rights. Anyhow, seamen are gregarious men. The thought of occupying the abandoned ship must, at the least, have been alarming. Only the salvage money which could come out of it, as the row-boat ducked and rolled on the Atlantic swell, can have driven him on. He trusted that Captain Morehouse, with his skeleton crew, could shadow him. Tough seaman though he was he must have been frightened. If he wasn't, he would have lacked the will to bring the *Mary Celeste* into harbour.

The reckless derelict, with an aimless wheel, was throwing about in a sea which, although the wind had dropped, was still angry. In the rowboat, Deveau had to time his approach to her. In a drunken lurch she could so easily have sunk him. As one of his men grabbed at her sides he flung himself out of the rowboat on to the chains. The other two followed. Together they hoisted the rowboat through a gap in the rail on to the deck. God knows, they might well need it later.

Deveau had seen the mess aboard her before but it was enough to break a seaman's heart. The essential tidiness of a ship is the key to survival. With two men, he had to get her under control. He put her wheel into the wind, using what sail she had left to get her on course. He put his men to the pumps until, an hour or two later, she was dry. He set about putting the broken binnacle, with its compass, in order. He found a spare trysail which he rigged as a foresail. He drilled holes in the galley to clear the seawater out of her.

None of them could sleep in beds which were soaking wet. They brought out the mattresses, the blankets and the sheets to dry them in the sun-starved sky. In their fatigue, they made no attempt to light the stove in the main cabin.

They found pleny of food and water, of a kind. Deveau threw overboard a three-quarters full bag of flour which was seeped in seawater. They ate casked salt beef.

They cooked potatoes, and perhaps onions, on a hissing galley fire. They slept, when they had a chance, in their own clothes. Three of them had to divide the watches, four hours at a time, twenty-four hours a day. They had to struggle, all of them, for two days before the ship was enough to rights to make any headway.

Deveau comforted himself that she was staunch and sound. Although he only had a first mate's ticket, he had mastered a brig before. His hope, as he and his men struggled to raise sail, was that it might be the beginning of a new career for him.

At first they were blessed, in Atlantic language, with reasonably fine weather. *Dei Gratia* was able to keep her in sight, and spoke to her several times. Little by little, the tired men aboard *Mary Celeste* brought her into some sort of trim. Uncomfortable as she was, she was sailing fair. Her mother ship was close beside her.

Deveau said afterwards that, standing at the wheel, he often wondered what had happened to her crew. Not an imaginative man, as so many others without his personal experience showed to be, he could only assume that 'there was a panic from the belief that the vessel had more water in her than she had, as afterwards proved'. At the time it was hardly surprising that, worn-out with nothing of a crew, he was only concerned with getting the ship into Gibraltar. In the Court of Enquiry, he was encountered again and again about his ship's positions, why he did not keep the log day by day, why he didn't choose this landfall or that. The very fact that he brought the *Mary Celeste* in, against all the odds, should have been enough to silence the lawyers.

His was a superb maritime achievement. 'We had fair weather at first and, until we got into the Straits when it came on a storm, so that I dare not make the Bay, but laid to under Ceuta, and afterwards on the Spanish Coast to the East.' The simple statement by the simple seaman to the Court of Enquiry in Gibraltar hid so much. Three sleepless men, red-eyed with weariness, had navigated a vessel into port which hadn't been overcrewed when it was in good order with eight. He had lost contact with the *Dei Gratia* in the heavy weather. But he brought in *Mary Celeste* a mere twenty-four hours after her.

He might have expected to receive the congratulations of everybody on the Rock. The only congratulations he had was when he reported to his Captain. Aboard the

Dei Gratia, Captain Morehouse watched him come in. He put out a boat to welcome him, only to find that his first mate had already come aboard his own ship. Turning back, he hurried to shake his hand. 'I congratulated him on his having succeeded in bringing in the ship, and he answered: "Yes, but I don't know that I would attempt it again." He appeared very fatigued and sleepy. "If a storm had come on, there would have been very great risk to both of us. I consider there was considerable, I may say very great risk to our lives and property." ' In evidence, he spoke the bare truth of the business. From the hour when, according to custom, the *Mary Celeste* had notice of arrest nailed to her mainmast, David Reed Morehouse and his men were subject to stony suspicion.

In early optimism, on Saturday, December 14, 1872, Morehouse sent a cablegram to the brokers in New York: 'FOUND FOURTH AND BROUGHT HERE MARY CELESTE ABANDONED SEAWORTHY ADMIRALTY IMPOST NOTIFY ALL PARTIES TELEGRAPH OFFER OF SALVAGE.' On the same day, the American Consul in Gibraltar, Horatio J. Sprague, telegraphed the Board of Underwriters in New York: 'BRIG MARY CELESTE HERE DERELICT IMPORTANT SEND POWER ATTORNEY TO CLAIM HER FROM ADMIRALTY COURT.' He sent another message to the American Consul at Genoa, where *Mary Celeste* was bound with her cargo of alcohol, for the lading bill. Initially, they all believed that the affair would be rapidly resolved.

Captain Morehouse and his men, who had come to Gibraltar for orders, with a cargo of petroleum aboard, could proceed on their voyage in the *Dei Gratia* with the promise of perhaps half the salvage money of $17,400 on *Mary Celeste*'s hull and freight interests and half the value of the cargo, insured in sterling, said to be worth £6,522 3s. od.

Salvors and underwriters reckoned without Mr Solly Flood. Solly Flood Esquire had the splendid title of 'Advocate and Proctor for the Queen in Her Office of

Admiralty'. He seems also to have been the prototype bureaucrat. More than anyone else it was he who, with the industry of a dung beetle, advanced *Mary Celeste* into history. A lazier official might have been glad to be rid of the business. It might easily have happened that the story of the ship with no one aboard her could have passed as unmemorably as other mysteries of the sea. Mr Solly Flood wasn't having that. In his capacity as 'Advocate and Proctor for the Queen in Her Office of Admiralty,' this was his Humpty-Dumpty moment of Glory. He made the most of it. A big fish in a small pond, he humphed, haggled and hawed until the world stopped, looked and listened.

He destroyed all hope that the *Mary Celeste* would be quickly released from the custody of the Court. Thomas Vecchio, the Marshal, said that, 'since she has been in my arrest, no less than five men, by advice of the Port Authorities, have been aboard her, with two anchors in the water and one ready to drop.'

The story of the seamen, who reported to the port authorities at Gibraltar, seems so convincing. It didn't seem so at the time to the people who were on the Rock. In fairness to Solly Flood, there are factors which deny explanation. The mystery of the *Mary Celeste*, thanks largely to him, remains.

4. THE SUSPICIONS OF MR. SOLLY FLOOD

Suspicion is not evidence. But the atmosphere of suspicion which generated on the Rock within a few days of *Mary Celeste*'s arrival undoubtedly influenced the whole conduct of the subsequent enquiry. The mood cannot be expressed in factual terms. The facts were never established. In this chapter I have endeavoured to seek a reconstruction of the dialogue between personalities in the case, people tapping their noses, talking behind locked ship's cabins and closed doors.

It may possibly give a more significant clue to the tensions, the controversies, the idiosyncrasies of the people involved in that strange affair a hundred years ago. I cannot know their exact words. Where I have left out their names they are people of my own invention, although I am in little doubt that such types were there. Where I have used names they are the real people whose opinions and correspondence are confirmed by the records. In the next chapter I have analysed my own impressions. Here's the stuff of the drama:

In mess kit, a Royal Naval Captain and a Major in the Royal Engineers are sitting over the port in one of the clubs on the Rock.

R.N. CAPTAIN: Have you heard about the brigantine - hermaphrodite brig, half-brig, or whatever it is that the Yankees call it – lying in the Harbour? The story is that they found her, sound as a bell, sailing the Atlantic, with not a soul aboard.

R.E. MAJOR: Jolly odd, I'd say, sir.

31

R.N. CAPTAIN: Odd's right. I'm told that she had a full cargo of crude alcohol, stuff for the Iti's to fortify their wretched wines.

R.E. MAJOR: I'd say that it's a Yankee trick.

R.N. CAPTAIN: The gossip on the Rock is that this feller Captain Morehouse, the master of this Nova Scotian vessel who found her, and Captain whatever-his-name-is, who abandoned her, were friends. It's being said, I don't know how much truth there is in it, that they dined together in New York the night before they sailed.

R.E. MAJOR (*nosing his port*): Anything, sir, can happen in New York. I recall an embarrassing incident I had there with a certain woman who shall, of course, be nameless....

He is interrupted by the entrance of a plump and pompous man, taking a pinch of snuff and dusting it off with a large handkerchief, who joins them at the table. He is Mr F. Solly Flood, Gibraltar's Attorney General. He is an Irishman in his middle sixties.

R.N. CAPTAIN: Ah, here's the man who knows all about it. Join us for a glass of port, sir.

Mr Flood is not unwilling.

R.N. CAPTAIN (*passing the wine*): We've been talking about the Yankee ship, with no one aboard her.

R.E. MAJOR: Damned fishy business.

SOLLY FLOOD: You are right, sir. I mean to get to the bottom of it. As you know, an enquiry is proceeding.

R.N. CAPTAIN: It's being said that, when she was found, there was a half-finished breakfast, still warm, on the saloon table?

SOLLY FLOOD: Fancies, sir, proliferate on the Rock. I am concerned with facts. I am dissatisfied with the account I have been given of the finding of this unmanned ship. My advice is that the tale I have been told by the people who have filed a claim for salvage – they have telegraphed New York to that effect – is unbelievable.

R.E. MAJOR: Stuff and nonsense. Must be.

R.N. CAPTAIN: No ship could have sailed for nine days – that's their story, isn't it? – with no one aboard her.

SOLLY FLOOD: I'm ordering down a diver. And when I have completed my own enquiries – which I can tell you confidentially, gentlemen, arouse my deepest suspicions – I shall be obliged if you will come aboard with me so that I may have the benefit of your expert judgement.

R.E. MAJOR: Delighted, I'm sure.

R.N. CAPTAIN: Mutiny?

SOLLY FLOOD: Or conspiracy. Perhaps both. Your health, gentlemen.

Mr Solly Flood raises his glass. With a change of passage, he is raising an admonitory finger in the Vice Admiralty Court. He is now in wig and gown. He is interrogating Captain Morehouse.

CAPTAIN MOREHOUSE: That's the way it was.

SOLLY FLOOD: As an experienced master in sail, have you ever known anything like it happen before?

CAPTAIN MOREHOUSE: Can't say I have.

SOLLY FLOOD: You were very fortunate to encounter such a prize.

CAPTAIN MOREHOUSE: I took a chance, undermanning my own vessel, to bring her in.

SOLLY FLOOD: To your financial advantage – as you hope.

CAPTAIN MOREHOUSE: It's the law of the sea.

SOLLY FLOOD (*irascibly*): It's the law of Her Majesty the Queen, in her Office of Admiralty, you have to convince, captain.

Mr Solly Flood turns away.

SOLLY FLOOD (*to the Court*): Enquiries are still proceeding. Your Lordship, I request a further adjournment.

HIS LORDSHIP: The court is adjourned.

C

A rowboat puts across the harbour to the Mary
Celeste. *Aboard are Mr Solly Flood, the R.N. Captain and the R.E. Major.* They clamber aboard.*

*The party come over the side of the vessel in the gap
where the rail has been lifted, and still not replaced.*

SOLLY FLOOD: Our investigation leads us first to the captain's cabin. Follow me, gentlemen.

*Puffing and blowing with officious importance, he
leads them aft in single file. In passing, the R.N. Captain taps the battened windows in the deck housing.*

R.N. CAPTAIN: She must have run into heavy weather.
SOLLY FLOOD: We shall see, sir.

*The R.N. Captain passes to look at the binnacle
which Deveau has lashed into place again.*
*Mr Solly Flood leads them into the gloom of the
cabin. He strikes a match, and lights a paraffin lamp
on the wall. The appearance of the cabin is much the
same as it was when Oliver Deveau came aboard for
the first time. The Log Slate has been seized. The Captain's bed has been made. But the pathetic damp rem-
nants of Captain Briggs and his family – 'sheet music
on the rosewood melodeon, two ladies' hats, night
shirt, a doll, a fan, two ladies' breast pins, a crinoline'
– lie where Deveau found them. Triumphantly, Mr
Solly Flood indicates on a narrow shelf a small phial
containing oil for use with a sewing machine, a
thimble and a reel of cotton.*

SOLLY FLOOD: All, you'll notice, in the perpendicular position. We have the statement of the witness, Deveau, that

---

* The real names of the British officers who went aboard with Mr
Solly Flood were Capt. Fitzroy, R.N., *HMS Minatour*; Capt. Adeane
R.N., *H.M.S. Agincourt*; Capt. Dowell, C.B., R.N., *H.M.S. Hercules*;
Capt. Vansittart, R.N., *H.M.S. Sultan,* and Col. Gaffan, RE. In sub-
stance what they agreed is told here.

he was much too busy putting the ship to rights – took him three days, he said – to tidy the cabin. So much for the theory that she met heavy weather.

R.N. CAPTAIN: I understood that the binnacle was stove in.

SOLLY FLOOD: The witness Deveau said that they lashed it back to bring her in.

R.N. CAPTAIN: So she did meet heavy weather.

SOLLY FLOOD: With all respect, sir, I suggest that there's another explanation.

He dives under the captain's bunk, and triumphantly produces the sword. Drawing it from the scabbard, he indicates rusty stains on the blade to the R.E. Major.

SOLLY FLOOD: In my opinion, sir, blood!

R.E. MAJOR (*taking the sword*): Could be blood, sir.

SOLLY FLOOD: The blade has been cleaned with lemon to disguise it. I intend to have a chemical analysis.

R.N. CAPTAIN: She has a cargo of alcohol. Did the crew get at the liquor?

SOLLY FOOD: I should like you now, sir, to look at the hold.

They leave the cabin, and go forward.

R.E. MAJOR (*as they come on deck*): It's obvious that those Yankees have been up to something. I had an unfortunate experience myself in New York some years ago. . . .

R.N. CAPTAIN (*killing his story*): Let's look at the cargo.

He stares down into the forehold, where the barrels of alcohol are ranged in neat rows, fore and aft. Laying himself on his face, he sniffs. Mr Solly Flood looks on complacently.

R.N. CAPTAIN: There's a barrel here which looks as if it's been broached, or started. You could be right, Mr Flood.

SOLLY FLOOD: I thought you'd agree with me. But that's not all.

Mr Solly Flood leads them to the starboard top-gallant rail. He points out to them a scar in the wood.

SOLLY FLOOD: Undoubtedly made by an axe. And observe, gentlemen, these marks on the deck, washed by the sea. Undoubtedly, blood. And there's a strange mark – you can see it if you lean over the bows – two or three feet above the water line. It's evident that the wood has recently been cut away from the outer planking to suggest that she was unsafe.

R.N. CAPTAIN: All the signs of mutiny.

R.E. MAJOR: It's a damned fishy business, that's what I say.

Mr Solly Flood is writing, with a dip pen, at his desk. It is one of his many letters to the Board of Trade in London. Hanging his pen on his cheek, he reads an extract from it to himself with satisfaction.

SOLLY FLOOD: 'My own theory or guess is that the crew got at the alcohol, and in the fury of drunkenness murdered the Master, whose name was Briggs, his wife and child and the chief mate; and that they did, sometime between the 25th November and the 5th December, escape on board some vessel bound for some North or South American port or the West Indies.'

More than content with what he has written, he subscribes himself aloud.

'I remain, sir, your most obedient servant, Advocate and Proctor for the Queen, Frederick Solly Flood.'

While Mr Solly Flood is reporting to London, Mr Horatio Sprague, the American Consul in Gibraltar, is reporting to Washington on 'the sad and silent mystery of the sea'. He is a thin man, an 'Uncle Sam', very different from the explosive Mr Solly Flood. His spidery cursive hand indicates his dry determination that the record shall be kept cool and straight. An American naval captain, Captain R. W. Shufeldt, of the U.S.S. Plymouth, has also examined the derelict. He dismisses with contempt the British theory that there has been mischief aboard. He is dispatching Captain Shufeldt's comments to the Secretary of State. In Gibraltar, Captain Shufeldt himself has made no secret of what he thinks of British suspicions, and British innuendoes. Captain Shufeldt is at a silver-furnished dinner table. The ladies have retired and the men – the R.N. Captain, the R.E. Major, Mr Solly Flood, and Mr Horatio Sprague – are joined over the port at the head of the mahogany board. The serving officers are in mess kit, the others in full evening dress.

CAPTAIN SHUFELDT (*to the R.N. Captain*): I reject the idea of mutiny, sir, because there is no evidence of violence about the decks, or in the cabins.

R.N. CAPTAIN (*with ill-concealed dislike*): With respect, captain, you can't explain away the damage to the planks on the bows. The injury has been sustained recently, and couldn't have been affected by weather.

CAPTAIN SHUFELDT (*angrily interrupting him*): The damage about the bows of the brig, sir, is no more than splinters made in the bending of the planks, afterwards forced off by the action of the sea.

Mr Solly Flood, who has restlessly kept his silence, butts in.

SOLLY FLOOD: What you can't explain is the gash in the wood of the rail, the barrels of alcohol which were broached, and the bloody sword.

CAPTAIN SHUFELDT: You have a lively imagination, Mr Flood.

R.E. MAJOR (*vaguely*): Myself, I still think it's an odd business. I remember, as if it were yesterday....

SOLLY FLOOD (*ignoring him, and wagging a finger to Captain Shufeldt*): Mark my words, captain. It won't be long before the survivors of the *Mary Celeste* are reported.

CAPTAIN SHUFELDT (*irritably*): I sincerely hope so – to put an end to an unpleasant business.

HORATIO SPRAGUE (*drily*): I assure you, Mr Flood, that Washington already has the matter in hand. Instructions have been issued to our Customs' officers to watch every point of entry. If any of the crew of the brig are alive, you may rest upon it that they will be intercepted.

SOLLY FLOOD: And we shall uncover a story of murder and mutiny on the high seas.

HORATIO SPRAGUE (*patiently*): I can't disprove you, Mr Flood. But I have known the missing master, Captain Briggs, for many years, and he has always born the highest character for seamanship and correctness. He is known as a Christian and an intelligent and active shipmaster.

SOLLY FLOOD: Bejabees, what's that got to do with it if he's got a murthering crew?

CAPTAIN SHUFELDT: There's not the slightest sign aboard of violence.

R.N. CAPTAIN: Nine barrels of the cargo of alcohol dry?

CAPTAIN SHUFELDT: They couldn't drink crude alcohol.

R.N. CAPTAIN: Seamen have. Nine barrels out of seventeen hundred and one are empty.

R.E. MAJOR (*vaguely*): My opinion is that it's mutiny.

CAPTAIN SHUFELDT (*rising to his feet in protest*): And my opinion, sir, in this unfortunate business, is that you British are casting discredit, without a fragment of evidence, on our American maritime marine.

Weeks after the enquiry has been dragging on, Captain Winchester, half-owner of the Mary Celeste, *arrives in Gibraltar from New York. Angry at the delay and procrastinations of English justice, he explodes.*

WINCHESTER: I am a citizen of the United States. I am told that I am of English descent. But, if I knew where the English blood was, I'd open a vein, and let it out.

Captain Winchester isn't the only one who is fed up.

CAPTAIN MOREHOUSE: To hell with them. We've got a cargo to deliver in Genoa. We can't leave the *Dei Gratia* rotting here. Take her off quickly, Deveau, and I'll stay here to fight the salvage claim.

The Vice Admiralty Court is buzzing again. Oliver Deveau is again in the witness box. Mr Solly Flood is again cross-examining him.

SOLLY FLOOD: Mr Deveau, you have caused the court considerable inconvenience and delay.

DEVEAU: I had orders to deliver our cargo to Genoa.

SOLLY FLOOD: While the enquiry on the derelict is still in progress.

DEVEAU: The *Dei Gratia* wasn't under arrest.

HIS LORDSHIP: (*severely*): Your conduct, in departing from Gibraltar while this court is sitting, is most reprehensible.

DEVEAU (*defensively*): Captain Morehouse was here all the time.

HIS LORDSHIP: It is very strange that the master of the *Dei Gratia*, who knows little or nothing to help the investigation, has remained here while you and the crew who boarded the derelict were allowed to go away.

DEVEAU: I'd already told the court all I knew.

HIS LORDSHIP: Yes, yes, Mr Deveau. But you must have known, or guessed, that there are certain matters which have been brought to my notice respecting this vessel, the *Mary Celeste*, matters on which I have already very decidedly expressed my opinion, which make it desirable, and even necessary, that further investigation should take place. . . .

Copies of the Gibraltar Chronicle are coming off an old flat-bed machine. After three months, the sensational developments which people on the Rock expected have not materialised. The court reluctantly awards salvage to the master and crew of the Dei Gratia. In the privacy of his cabin Captain Morehouse expostulates with Oliver Deveau.

CAPTAIN MOREHOUSE: Seventeen hundred pounds. That's all we get out of it. A miserable fifth of the total value of the ship, and her cargo. Never again.

DEVEAU (*quietly*): They've decided that we're liars.

The two men look at each other enigmatically. Captain Morehouse spits.

5. THE RIDDLES

It is a pity that the transcript of the proceedings in the Vice Admiralty Court 'against the ship or vessel supposed to be called *Mary Celeste*' only contains the statements of the witnesses. It is a form of recording evidence which is still employed. But, without the questions which were put by counsel, the mood of the enquiry is only partly revealed. It was certainly more acrimonious than it seems in the documents of the case which are preserved in the Supreme Court at Gibraltar.

It is also evident that the controversy outside the court was even more heated than what went on within. The story of *Mary Celeste* is only partly told in the mystery surrounding what happened to her master and crew. The clash of personalities on the Rock when she was brought in has a significance of its own.

Students of the case have tended to concentrate their attention on clues found aboard the ship – a broken halliard, a scar on a rail, a rusty sword, a broached cask of alcohol. What I find equally intriguing is that when the brig was under arrest, locked with two anchors and a third in reserve, the British, led by Mr Solly Flood, were convinced that they recognised all the signs of a conspiracy. The Americans, led by their consul, Mr Horatio Sprague, were equally confident that there was an innocent explanation. It is also important to underline that during the eighty-seven days, from December 13, 1872, until March 10, all parties confidently expected that survivors would turn up; or that, at any rate, another ship would report news of them. In court, Mr Solly Flood had no hesitation in representing himself as the guardian of the interests of

41

the missing captain, Benjamin Briggs, as well as of Queen Victoria.

The enigmatic character in the drama is the one man who apparently told less than he could have done. David Morehouse, the captain and part-owner of the *Dei Gratia*, had most to gain from the derelict. Henry Peter Pisani, his advocate, was claiming on his behalf; and for 'the owners, officers and crew', as the 'asserted salvors'. Morehouse was a Nova Scotian, born on March 2, 1838, who went to sea when he was sixteen years old, and became a captain at the age of twenty-one. He had a reputation as a navigator.

During the court proceedings the judge remarked that, in the first instance, he had understood that the captain of the *Dei Gratia* was not to be examined at all. In the event, he was one of the last witnesses. His evidence was laconic. There is a suggestion of truculence. If I am right it was not surprising.

On December 23, exasperated by the procrastinations of the court, he had ordered his first mate, Oliver Deveau, to sail *Dei Gratia* with her cargo of petroleum out of Gibraltar to Genoa, while he himself stayed behind to watch their interests. The Judge, Sir James Cochrane, was scathing: 'The conduct of the Salvors in going away as they have done has in my judgement been more reprehensible and may probably influence the decision as to their claim for remuneration for their services and it appears very strange why the captain of the *Dei Gratia* who knows little or nothing to help the investigation should have remained here while the first mate and the crew who boarded the *Celeste* and brought her here should have been allowed to go away as they have done.'

When Deveau returned, after an adjournment of the court to wait for him, he didn't endear the crew of the *Dei Gratia* any more by reporting that Charles Lund, one of the seamen who had sailed with him in the derelict to Gibraltar had damaged his back at Genoa and wasn't fit to appear again.

Captain Morehouse's conduct, whatever impression he made on the court, was understandable. It was in the best tradition of the sea that, when he put his men aboard the derelict, he remained on his own deck. It was no wonder that a man accustomed to giving orders resented official and officious delays. Time was money, especially to a sailing ship's captain. He reckoned that he had lost four days bringing in *Mary Celeste*. It was reasonable to see the lawyers to hell, and land his own cargo in Italy.

But in his own evidence, and his crew's evidence, there seems to be one remarkable omission. It is a matter which, unless the transcript is faulty, was never raised in court at all. In retrospect, it is astonishing that years passed before it came out.

In 1927, J. G. Lockhart, a responsible naval historian (on the English side) told that Morehouse and Briggs, the master of the *Mary Celeste*, were old acquaintances, and had actually dined together in New York on the night before the brig sailed. His authority, he claimed, was Mrs Morehouse, the captain's wife. In 1956, Hanson W. Baldwin, the distinguished writer (on the American side) went much further.

'It is also known that the brigantine *Dei Gratia* of Nova Scotian registry, was in New York loading cargo while the *Celeste* prepared for her voyage into history. Skipper Briggs and Skipper Morehouse were old friends; they had encountered each other in many of the ports of the seven seas. Morehouse, like Briggs, was part-owner and master of his ship, and sometimes took his wife along on his cruises. Mr Briggs and Mrs Morehouse, like their husbands, were also old friends and had met at ports-of-call in various parts of the world. So it was natural that the two masters should see something of each other while their ships were loading – the *Celeste* with the barrels of alcohol, the *Dei Gratia* with a mixed cargo (apparently) for Mediterranean ports. Some say that Briggs and Morehouse even had dinner together at the old Astor House the night before the *Celeste* sailed, but there is no evidence of this and no certainty that the two skippers did meet.'

That Morehouse knew Briggs, working from the same ports in the same sort of trading ships, seems more than likely. They had loaded on the same wharves in New York, and sailed the same course within days of each other. Men with identical interests tend to mix together. Then why not a word about it in the examination of the salvage claim? Morehouse, looking through his glass, even at six miles away, must have made a good guess that he spied *Mary Celeste*. His first mate said that they hadn't sighted another brig in twenty days at sea. Seamen take pride in recognising another sail, rather as motorists know their neighbours' cars. Yet it seems that the captain never confided to his own crew that he knew the wayward ship, or her master. His men, who might have been expected to use their own eyes, were silent.

In ordinary circumstances it was surely the first thing that a man would tell; that he had identified the ship and that he knew her master. Horatio Sprague, the American Consul in Gibraltar, said that he knew Captain Briggs well. While he said nothing about Captain Morehouse, it is possible that he might have had an acquaintance with him, too. It is a fancy of mine that the rumour that the two skippers were friends reached the Rock during the enquiry. It probably didn't; otherwise it seems incredible that the vital question was not raised in court. Nevertheless, it is worth adding that such omissions, in the search for fact, are not unusual; especially in the formality and strain of legal evidence.

The Queen's Advocate came, as I think, precipitately to the conclusion that this was a case of mutiny and murder on the high seas. He based his theory, supported by British officers, on 'a bloodstained sword', and a broached cargo of alcohol. The crude alcohol, if the crew had drunk it, would have blinded them, and probably sent them to oblivion. They would anyhow have been too incapacitated for mutiny, never mind murder. The bloodstained sword, on which Mr Flood placed so much faith as a clue, and which he believed had been cleaned with lemon to conceal dark deeds, was thought later to be merely rusted. His disappointment is revealed in that the chemical analysis of the results was not disclosed until fourteen years later. Of course, the examination was inadequate in modern laboratory terms. Solly Flood was officiously playing his part as an amateur detective. It was almost certainly a false trail. But there remains a fragment or two of rust for reflection.

Hanson Baldwin, in explanation of the sword, writes: 'Briggs had been sailing the seas too long to be a great hand for souvenirs, but he had the common liking for the old and the rare, and somewhere in his cabin he had stowed away an old sword "of Italian make" with the cross of Savoy (described by others as a cross of Navarre) on the hilt, which he had picked up on a previous voyage while visiting an old battlefield near the head of the Adriatic Sea.'

From that it is difficult to conclude that there wasn't blood on it, sometime, somewhere. Anyhow, why had Briggs brought it aboard? People often have souvenirs littering their homes. Briggs had a house in Maine where he could conveniently have left it. Then why did he deliberately introduce it aboard *Mary Celeste* along with his wife's melodeon and sewing machine? He had never sailed in the ship before. What did he think that he wanted it for? Most captains at that time carried pistols. No pistol was found aboard the abandoned ship.

I believe that the Queen's Advocate, who from all the evidence looks like a silly old busybody, could have discovered, if he had had the wit, so much more. I would give an eye-tooth, if I could step back in time, to ask Captain Morehouse if he had ever heard of Captain Briggs. I would have liked to measure the man whose story, so it seems to me, is so pat. My own guess is that a conspiracy is not acceptable, although not inconceivable. The witnesses from the *Dei Gratia* were consistent. It might be added that they were almost too consistent; not the way eyewitnesses usually are, but the way of people with a brief. None of them contradicted each other. There was a slight difference of opinion between Oliver Deveau and the second mate, John Wright, about whether the brig showed evidence of having a ship's boat. In retrospect it seems negligible. She almost certainly did have a yawl, on chocks amidships, which was found missing. She seems to have sailed from her home port, irresponsibly, without a longboat. The story is that her longboat was damaged in harbour. The davits in the stern were found bound with a spar.

Latterly my belief is that Mr Solly Flood dismissed his theory of mutiny and murder. It was, anyhow, thinly based. Increasingly, he suspected collusion. It was so extraordinary that a ship, 'staunch and sound', with six months provisions aboard, could have been abandoned by her crew with such obvious haste.

He quickly followed one letter to the Board of Trade in London with another, dated Gibraltar, 23 January, 1873:

'Sir,
I beg leave to supplement my letter of the 22nd inst. by enclosing an extract from so much of the log of the Dei Gratia as is necessary to show the position of that vessel on and from the 24th November to the day when she met the Mary Celeste on the 5th of December from which it will appear that the wind during the whole of that time was more or less from the North, that she was during the whole of that time on the Port tack, and that consequently it seems incredible that the Mary Celeste should have run during the same period a distance of 7' 54E at least upon the starboard tack, under which tack she was when met by the Dei Gratia.

'*These circumstances seem to me to lead to the conclusion that – although no entry in the Log or on the
slate of Mary Celeste later than 8 a.m. on the 25th November is to be found, she had in fact not been abandoned
till several days afterwards, and probably also that she was
abandoned much further to the Eastward than the spot
where she was found.*

I have etc.
Fredk. Solly Flood
H.M.S. *Advocate General & Proctor for the Queen
in Her Office of Admiralty & Attorney General for
Gibraltar.*

The implication of the letter was that Morehouse and
his crew were telling less than truth; that they had not
found the derelict on the date they claimed in the position
they claimed. Mr Flood was the more inclined to suspect
mischief because the *Dei Gratia* had sailed for Genoa,
under the command of the first mate, without previous
consultation with the authorities, which meant him. He
presumed that Captain Morehouse was deliberately remov-
ing a witness with a view to concealing information from
the court. He was also supported in his opinion by the
affidavit of John Austin, the port's surveyor of shipping.
He enclosed Austin's report in his letter to London. It
was at least critical of the evidence of the crew of the
Dei Gratia.

Dei Gratia's story was that she had had heavy weather.
In his own evidence Captain Morehouse said 'it had been
blowing very hard for seven or eight days previous but on
that morning, morning of the fourth, commenced to
moderate'. The wind had dropped but the seas, he said,
were still high when he put his men aboard the derelict.
Mary Celeste, sailing four days ahead of him, had probably tasted the same weather.

Yet John Austin, when he examined the ship, could not
believe it. She had not, in his opinion, encountered bad

weather. '*On the starboard side of the main cabin was the chief mate's cabin, on a little bracket in which I found a small phial of oil for a sewing machine in its proper perpendicular position, a reel of cotton for such a machine, and a thimble. If they had been there in bad weather then they would have been thrown down or carried away. The chief mate's bedding was perfectly dry, and had not been wetted or affected by water. In the lower drawer under the bedplace were a quantity of loose bits of iron and two unbroken panes of glass which wd. have been broken to pieces had the Vessel encountered any seriously bad weather.*' Earlier in his numbered report, listed as points 22–23, he wrote: '*The forward deckhouse was lighted by two windows on each side, those on the port side were covered by a thin sliding shutter. The after window on the starboard side was uncovered. None of the shutters or the windows were injured in the slightest degree. Some of them must have been greatly injured or wholly destroyed if the vessel had experienced very bad weather.*'

The surveyor's evidence need not be accepted in its entirety. Oliver Deveau had stated in court that he had dried out the beds. He, or one of his men, might well have set up the phial of oil, the reel of cotton, and the thimble. One wonders why the questions were not asked. In so many ways the enquiry was cursed with incompetence. It may be that it was also limited by lack of information.

They had the telegraph; but what they hadn't got was instant communication in detail with the rest of the world. The story of the *Mary Celeste* might not be the mystery it is if people could have talked to each other more quickly. I have had to guess, on the reports of others, that Briggs and Morehouse were friends; an important fact which any newspaperman could discover in a few hours today. I can only guess the news which reached Gibraltar at the time the enquiry was going on.

Did they know that, in New York, some were saying that she sailed under false colours? The story came out in the *New York Sun* on March 12, 1873, almost immediately after the enquiry in Gibraltar was ended:

THE ABANDONED SHIP: NO MUTINY BUT A SCHEME TO DEFRAUD THE INSURANCE COMPANY.

The stories in regard to the desertion of the Brig Mary Celeste, with another ship recently found abandoned in mid-ocean, are not credited in Custom House circles. Mention is made of several suspicious circumstances to show that more selfish motives than the revolting of sailors and the slaying of their officers might have prompted the abandonment of the vessel. A Sun reporter was informed that the Mary Celeste had been improperly cleared and sailed under false colors after going out of this port. It was charged that deception was resorted to for the purpose of getting her registered as an American vessel. She was built at Parrsboro, (this is incorrect) *Nova Scotia in 1861, and formerly sailed under the British flag, being known as the Amazon.*

In 1870, (error), *she took her present name, and was afterwards registered as American built. Deputy Surveyor Abeel discovered the deception a few months ago, and took measures to seize the brig on her next arrival in port....'*

There was more to it. Enough that the sheer legitimacy of *Mary Celeste* was in doubt. Nobody was even sure about her name. She was christened *Amazon* when she was built in Canada. She first sailed under the British flag. After she ran ashore on Cow Bay it is even said that her new owners renamed her *Mary Sellars*. J. H. Winchester & Co. of New York, the same whose chief appeared in the court at Gibraltar, denied hotly in the *New York Herald* that there was any truth in the assertion that his company was associated in a conspiracy; that 'the ship was correctly registered under the American flag and that published reports about the vessel being illegally cleared and sailing under a false flag, which originated with a Custom House official, are base fabrications, as

anyone interested in the matter can discover by referring
to the Custom House and the officers of the companies
which we are insured'.

There is no doubt that the company, which still
flourishes today, spoke with conviction. But, in the strange
case of *Mary Celeste*, did her half-owners know it all? It is
notable that, in the examination of James Henry Winchester, they pressed him about the cargo. It is evident
that Solly Flood was beginning to believe that when the
crew abandoned ship they had something valuable to take
with them. Even in the dry transcript of the court
proceedings Captain Winchester emerges as a strong
character.

'*I was at New York when the Mary Celeste sailed on her
last voyage. I know what cargo she had on board. It consisted of 1701 barrels of alcohol. One barrel in dispute
with thirty tons of stone ballast beneath the cargo. To my
knowledge she had no other cargo.... That is the whole
of the cargo. I saw it going aboard several times, and saw
no other cargo.... I knew Benj. S. Briggs, the master of
the Mary Celeste. I had known him for several years and
saw him write his name to the Bills of Lading. I was acting
as ship's husband on this occasion and had there been any
other cargo I should most likely have known of it. I have
no doubt whatever of the vessel being the Mary Celeste of
New York. I do not know whether she had a ship's mani-
fest when she left New York... When she sailed from
New York she had a chronometer aboard. It was a hired
one found by the master himself who sailed the vessel on
shares. I do not know whether she had a sextant and
quadrant.... The vessel loaded at Pier 44 East River about
one mile from my office. I used to go there once a day
three different days during the time she took in her cargo
... I do not think it is possible that there was any other
cargo or bullion or other valuables on board without my
knowing it, but still such a thing is possible. Briggs was in
charge ten or twelve days before the Mary Celeste sailed. I*

*do not know that he took any valuables on board without
my knowledge . . . I don't think that either Richardson (the
first mate) or the captain had any venture of their own on
board the Celeste as they had not private funds, but they
might have had a venture of someone else.'*

From a reading of all the evidence it is apparent that
there was doubt at the time on almost every count;
whether *Mary Celeste* was the brig she was described to
be; whether her cargo was all that it was meant to be;
whether *Dei Gratia* had found her in the position she said
she had; and even the authenticity of the backlog of the
Atlantic weather.

The theory of 'mutiny and murder' was succeeded by
the view that the master of the brig had entered into a
plot with another vessel, likely the *Dei Gratia*, to stage a
fake abandonment with the object of collecting salvage
money. The notion seemed not so far-fetched when none
could believe that Captain Briggs, his wife, daughter and
crew would never be heard of again.

It remains mysterious that the crew of the *Dei Gratia*
said that they didn't identify the brig until they boarded
her, and saw her log and slate. Perhaps her name was not
painted on her stern or sides, a rather improbable circumstance in a ship which had just been completely rebuilt
and refitted. As Deveau testified; 'the hull was apparently
new, the masts were good, the spars all right. . . . she was
seaworthy and almost a new vessel.' But neither is there
any evidence that she flew a national flag; and the detailed
inventory of the gear found aboard the ship makes no
mention that she even had one. The Vice Admiralty court
refers to her as the ship 'supposed to be *Mary Celeste*'.
Perhaps there was a residue of fact in the rumour about
her registration.

The damage to the timbers in her bows, and the cut in
the rail, are other enigmas. Captain Winchester said that
neither was there when she left New York. He declared
that the cut in the rail had been made 'by a severe blow

with a sharp instrument'. From his report, John Austin, Gibraltar's surveyor of shipping, appears not to have noticed it. But he was highly suspicious of the marks on the bows:

'*On approaching the vessel I found on the bow between two and three feet above the water line on the port side a long narrow strip of the edge of one of the outer planks under the cat-head cut away to the depth of about three eighths of an inch or about one inch and a quarter wide for a length of about 6 to 7 feet. This injury had been sustained very recently and could not have been affected by the weather and was apparently done by a sharp cutting instrument continuously applied through the whole length of the injury ... I found on the starboard bow but a little further from the stern of the vessel a precisely similar injury but perhaps an eighth or a tenth of an inch wider wh. in my opinion had been effected at the same time and by the same means and not otherwise.*'

Captain Winchester disagreed. His own opinion confirmed that of the American naval officer, Captain Shufeldt, who had diagnosed that the splints had spauled off the wood which had been steamed and bent to curve the bow when she was building.

In court there was nothing more to be said. On February 25, 1873, the American Consul Sprague wrote to the Department of State:

'*Since my last communication dated the 12th instant, on the subject of the Mary Celeste case, I have conferred with the Queen's Proctor in the Vice Admiralty Court regarding the formalities required by him for the restitution of the vessel to her original owners, and I am happy to add that I have succeeded in prevailing upon this law officer of the Crown the abandonment of his pretensions to have the said vessel bailed against any latent or other demands, beyond those of meeting the salvage claims and Court expenses. This formality has just been gone through, and the Mary Celeste has this evening been restored to her original owners, and she will now be in a position to proceed on her voyage to Genoa with her cargo of alcohol taken in at New York, thereby enabling her to earn her freight, and spare to the parties concerned much time and extra expenses. Of the missing Master and crew, nothing continues to be heard of them.'*

Consul Sprague's letter makes it abundantly clear what he thought of Mr Solly Flood. In the hope that the brig would be released earlier Captain Winchester had brought a new master, Captain Blatchford, out of New York. The master was waiting, from the beginning of February, to put a new crew aboard and refit her. But the Queen's Advocate General wouldn't budge; although it was costing her owners money every day *Celeste*, with a full cargo, idled in port. Captain Winchester left the Rock in a huff, and with empty pockets. He needed to raise money to meet his commitments on her. The Advocate General, still in hot pursuit of what he conceived was a Yankee conspiracy, was obdurate.

When he couldn't find the rats which he was convinced were waiting to be trapped he gave in with exasperating reluctance. It presumably gave him a certain satisfaction that the salvage money awarded by the court was only one fifth of the value of the vessel and her cargo. *Mary Celeste* was valued at $5,700.00 and her cargo at $39,943.00, total $42,673.00. The award was £1,700 to the master and crew of the *Dei Gratia*, the costs of the suit to be paid out of the property salved. The Judge further thought it proper to express the disapprobation of the Court that the master of the *Dei Gratia* had allowed the first mate, Oliver Deveau, to sail off while the analysis was being made of the supposed spots or stains of blood on the deck of the *Mary Celeste* and on the sword. Consequently, His Lordship decided that the costs of the analysis should be charged against the salvors. He could scarcely have made a meaner judgement. The crew of the *Dei Gratia* had expected a half, or at least a third. It was the usual custom in the law of the sea. But nothing was familiar in the case of *Mary Celeste*.

On March 10, 1873, Captain Winchester, on his return to New York, wrote to Consul Sprague apologising for his early departure. His wife was ill, he was under considerable expense, and his business at home was suffering through his absence. But the nub of the letter tells that, while he was in Gibraltar, 'a gentleman' came to him and told him that after the Judge and the Attorney General had used up every other pretence to cause delay and expense, they were going to arrest him for hiring the crew to make away with the officers. He goes on: 'From what you and everybody else in Gibraltar had told me about the attorney general, I did not know but he might do it as they seem to do just as they like.'

Not long after Captain Winchester wrote his own letter, Consul Sprague reported again to the Department of State. He recorded that *Mary Celeste* had cleared for Genoa. She arrived to discharge on March 21, 'having made the passage in eleven days, as against twenty-four days required by the *Dei Gratia* to perform a similar journey two months previously.' He might have wished, even though in an official letter he didn't care to write it, that he could have added more. What he must have said in private about the 'Limeys' was nobody's business.

Tempers at the time were high. Yet it might have been expected that the affair, after a few years, would have grumbled out of history. What happened was that it was only a beginning.

6. CONAN DOYLE'S FIRST
GREAT SHORT STORY

I cannot tell how Doctor Doyle got mixed in the business. What I know is that, as a young medical man, waiting hopefully for patients, he passed the empty hours in his consulting room trying his hand as a teller of tales. He belonged to a period which was remarkable for one of the great flowerings of English letters; especially in the art of the short story which now, alas, has almost faded. For a man of high imagination, the mystery of *Mary Celeste* must have had a special appeal.

It may be that he had heard something about her during a period in which he served as a ship's doctor. He could have seen a press clipping from a Gibraltar newspaper. I wish now that I had talked about it to him on the one occasion when I met him; but by then he was too immersed in spiritualism for more mundane conversation. I was also too young, and too naïve, to question him as I would today.

Conan Doyle, writing ten years after *Mary Celeste* was brought in, was not concerned, as Mr Sherlock Holmes would have been, with the facts of the case. What clearly intrigued him was how to explain an abandoned vessel with all her ship's boats aboard her. It appears that the maritime legend was already established that that was the way in which *Mary Celeste* was found. It was a challenge with consequences which Doyle could not possible have guessed – for himself and for the world.

A handsome man, over six feet tall with the flourishing waxed moustache which was fashionable in the period, smoking a Dublin-clay pipe, scratching with a dip pen on foolscap paper, he can hardly have hoped that his story would be published. An unknown doctor, how could he imagine that, in due time, he would be ranked as one of the great storytellers of a great age of storytellers?

His firstborn, 'J. Habakuk Jephson's Statement' was accepted, and duly appeared in the January, 1884, issue of the *Cornhill Magazine*, the most respected periodical of its day. He wrote it anonymously because professional etiquette required that, as a doctor, he shouldn't use his own name. Latterly, he published it again in a book titled *The Captain of the Polestar*, as A. Conan Doyle. He made no comment. By then, he had launched, ten years after it had happened, the everlasting riddle of *Mary Celeste*.

It is important to say that Doyle never claimed truth; nor, so far as I can find out, even commented on what he wrote. He was telling a story. But he named a ship which was a real ship, although he got the spelling of her name wrong. (It was a mistake that he may have picked up from Lloyd's list of 25th March, 1873, where it first occurred.) The latitude and longitude in which he told she was found abandoned fits fairly well with the evidence. He named correctly the brig *Dei Gratia* which encountered her. For the rest, he had no intention of worrying about detail. The vessel he describes has no resemblance to the actual ship. In his story Captain Briggs appears as 'Captain Tibbs'. I am sure that, in this context, Doyle would have had no objection to my giving Briggs and his ship their proper names. In his story he may well have changed them deliberately. But he was to be echoed later by so many others in the name of fact. Such is the magic of a great writer that even Holmes and Watson now seem almost true.

I have written Conan Doyle's invention in a style to match with others in this book. In the manner of his period he himself wrote at greater length. I write in mine, more briefly, what he passed on to posterity.

He began: 'In the month of December, in the year

1873, the British ship *Dei Gratia* steered into Gibraltar,
having in tow the derelict brigantine *Marie Celeste....*'
He went on to tell how an American medical man had
recorded that he was a passenger on *Mary Celeste*'s fateful voyage. He had only preserved silence so long, he
said, because he had been disgusted by the offensive dis-
belief of his own relations, and of a magistrate at Liverpool to whom he had confided his experience at the time.
But now, dying of consumption, he had decided to make
the matter public at last. It went on like this:

*No derelict now, Mary Celeste is bowling under full
sail, her cordage trim and neat, with a long white
furrow in her wake. In the captain's cabin, a man
of extraordinarily sinister appearance is furtively
examining a case of ship's chronometers which he has
open on the table. He is a tall gaunt man who appears
to be a quadroon. His curved aquiline nose and
straight lank hair shows the white strain; but he has
the dark restless eye, sensuous mouth and glittering
teeth of the African. His complexion is an unhealthy
yellow and his face is deeply pitted with small pox.
A large diamond winks in his shirt front. Horrifically,
he has lost all the fingers off his right hand. He is
studying the chronometers between thumb and palm.
He is distracted by the rattle of the deckhouse door
being thrown fully open, and the increased light it
throws below decks. He looks up momentarily with
'an utterly fiendish expression'. Then he is blotted
out by the shoulders of two other men entering the
little cabin. The newcomers are Captain Briggs and
Dr J. Habakuk Jephson. Dr Jephson, of the University of Harvard, is an eminent Broklyn specialist,
who has been severely wounded in the Civil War
and who is taking a sea passage to relieve consumption. The captain is a bluff and good-natured New
Englander. He is formally dressed in uniform with a*

brass telescope under his arm. Inside the cabin, he removes his cap and puts his telescope on the table.

CAPTAIN BRIGGS: Learning to sail my ship for me?

He sits down on the bench facing the quadroon whose menacing expression had now changed to an ingratiating smile.

CAPTAIN BRIGGS: At the start of the voyage, Mr Goring, I'm sure you won't mind my mentioning that the Captain's cabin is usually regarded as his sanctum.

SEPTIMIUS GORING (*half rising*): I didn't realise. Forgive my intrusion, sir. I'm afraid that I can only plead my ignorance of the usages of ship's life.

He speaks courteously, in the accent of the Deep South.

CAPTAIN BRIGGS: But you are interested in my chronometers. You stay right here, Mr Goring, and favour us with your company. As a matter of fact, it was a discussion about navigation which brought us below. I want to refer to one of the original works. You've met your fellow passenger, Dr Habakuk Jephson?

SEPTIMIUS GORING (*still smiling*): We caught a glimpse of each other in the shipping office.

CAPTAIN BRIGGS: Then you had better get to know each other better now. You are in adjoining cabins.

Septimius Goring leans across the cabin, and offers his maimed hand to the doctor who is standing shyly in the corner. Concealing his disgust with a consumptive cough, he takes it.

DR JEPHSON: A pleasure, I'm sure, sir.

CAPTAIN BRIGGS: Dr Jephson is an eminent medical man of the University of Harvard. Mr Septimius Goring comes, if I remember the passenger list aright, from New Orleans. But, no doubt, we'll all get to know each other better very soon.

SEPTIMIUS GORING: Are you travelling on medical business, Dr Jephson?

DR JEPHSON: In this case, my own. My own doctor thinks that rest and sea air may improve my pulmonary condition. And you?

SEPTIMIUS GORING (*evasively*): Call it a private business matter. (*to Captain Briggs*) You mentioned Maury's observations on Ocean currents.

CAPTAIN BRIGGS (*surprised*): Did I? It was indeed the actual work we came here to consult. You are interested in that, too?

SEPTIMIUS GORING: And also the variation of the compass. I have a little practical knowledge of mathematical instruments.

CAPTAIN BRIGGS: Um ... we must talk some more about it. Ah, here's my wife and our third passenger, Mr Harton, who is sailing with us to start a new life abroad.

Mrs Briggs, wearing a crinoline and carrying her 2-year-old baby in her arms, comes below with John Harton, a pleasant looking man in his twenties.

CAPTAIN BRIGGS: I think the rest of you have all met each other.

Exchanging smiles and greetings, they range themselves on both sides of the cabin table.

CAPTAIN BRIGGS: Now we're all together I think this calls for a celebration. We've got a bottle in the locker, haven't we, Sarah?

Mrs Briggs smiles her assent, and rocks the baby. Captain Briggs, in the confined quarters, twists a bottle out of a locker under his seat.

CAPTAIN BRIGGS: Perhaps Mr Harton will be good enough to get that new Sambo of ours to bring some glasses out of the pantry. Madeira, Mr Goring?

SEPTIMIUS GORING: Delighted, sir!

Dr Habakuk Jephson, who is sitting near to Mrs Briggs, speaks to the baby. The child is restless, and, putting his hand in his pocket, he produces a flattish black stone, with a hole through the middle of it, to amuse her. It is about three inches long, and an inch and a half broad at the middle. It has the exact appearance of a human ear. He shows it to the baby. At the sight of it Septimius Goring becomes powerfully excited.

SEPTIMIUS GORING: What's that?

DR JEPHSON: A trifling souvenir of mine from the war. I've carried it about in my pocket for years.

SEPTIMIUS GORING: May I look at it?

DR JEPHSON: Of course.

He passes it down the table. Septimius Goring examines it intently.

SEPTIMIUS GORING (*breathing heavily*): Where did you get it?

DR JEPHSON: If you're interested, it was pressed on me by an old negress who nursed me on a plantation when I was wounded with Grant's Army in the war. She took to me because she knew I was a keen abolitionist, and friend of the coloured folk. I've had it ever since. It's probably a meteorite.

While he is talking, John Harton returns to his seat in the cabin. He is followed by a negro carrying a tray of glasses. At the sight of the stone which Septimius Goring holds up for him to see, he drops the tray with a crash.

CAPTAIN BRIGGS (*angrily*): You careless dog.

MRS BRIGGS: Five of our precious glasses.

SEPTIMIUS GORING (*throwing the stone after the glasses*): Now pick that up.

The negro scrabbles for it eagerly. Picking it up, he rolls his eyes and clutches it to his chest.

NEGRO STEWARD: Who this belong to, massa?

DR JEPHSON (*quietly*): It's mine.

The steward hands it back to him with a deep obeisance and every sign of profound respect.

DR JEPHSON: That's how the old slave behaved who gave it to me. (*to Briggs*) It seems to be a sort of talisman which appeals to the dark race.

He drops the stone back into his pocket while Septimius Goring eyes him with hate.

CAPTAIN BRIGGS: You'd better not produce it again when there are glasses to drop. (*to the steward*) Go on, smartly, get some more.

The negro, still showing the whites of his eyes, returns.

CAPTAIN BRIGGS: I feared we'd have trouble with that steward. I had to sign him on, and another darkee on the quayside. At the last minute, inexplicably, two of our best and most reliable seamen didn't turn up. Still, we must make the best of what we've got.

He reaches for his hat and telescope.

CAPTAIN BRIGGS: My wife will look after you, gentlemen. I think I'll take a turn on deck.

DR JEPHSON: May I join you? My lungs need all the air they can get.

CAPTAIN BRIGGS: A pleasure, doctor.

In the general shuffle in the cabin, Septimius Goring seizes the opportunity to make another intense examination of the chronometers.
The Mary Celeste *made good sailing time. By dead*

reckoning about a hundred and seventy miles a day until about five days out, when the wind died away, and she lay in a long greasy swell, rustled by fleeting cats paws insufficient to fill the canvas. Even the presence of Captain Briggs' baby daughter didn't dispel the uneasy atmosphere which pervaded the ship. One of the dark seamen, half asleep at the wheel, is prodded awake by another who whispers conspiratorially in his ear. Captain Briggs, alone in his cabin, looks with a puzzled expression, at his chronometers. The three of them are registering different times. He picks up the case, puts it to his ear, shakes it, and shakes his own head.

Dr Jephson, desultorily reading a book in his bunk, can't keep his eyes away from a crack in the thin partition dividing his own from the cabin next door. Through the crack, Septimius Goring is stooping, with pencil and compasses, over what appears to be a chart. Dr Jephson slips out of his bunk. Wrapping a muffler about his neck, he quietly leaves his cabin, and goes up the companionway to the deck. Half way up the companionway, he is stopped by a loud explosion behind him. Coughing with the effort he turns back as Septimius Goring, with a smoking revolver in his hand, bumps into him.

SEPTIMIUS GORING (*his face twisted with emotion*): It's you! I thought I'd hit you. I was cleaning the revolver and one of the barrels I thought was unloaded went off through the partition into your cabin.

Calmly, Dr Jephson opens the door of his cabin. The ball has splintered a hole in the partition. He touches it.

DR JEPHSON: If I had been here it would have gone through my head. It was a lucky escape.

SEPTIMIUS GORING: My dear sir, I can't tell you how sorry I am.

DR JEPHSON: Think no more of it, I've been under fire before.

With the merest hint of suspicion in his expression, Dr Jephson retires again to his cabin, closing the door in Septimius Goring's face. Septimius Goring, staring after him at the closed door, stuffs his pistol in his pocket, and steals up to the open deck. The ship is veiled in darkness. The people on her decks are shadows. Dr Jephson is reading in the light of an oil lamp. He is disturbed by a sudden scurry.

CAPTAIN BRIGGS (*bursting, white-faced, into the doctor's cabin*): Have you seen my wife?

Dr Jephson sits in his bunk. Captain Briggs is bare-footed and coatless, with ruffled hair.

CAPTAIN BRIGGS: She's gone! My baby, too!

Leaving the cabin, he throws open the saloon door.

Sarah! Baby! Sarah!

His voice rises to a scream, and he rushes on deck.

CAPTAIN BRIGGS: Turn the ship about! My wife's missing ... Sarah!

Barefooted hands are heard rushing about the deck. Dr Jephson joins the captain.

DR JEPHSON: When did you last see her?

CAPTAIN BRIGGS: Within a quarter of an hour ... a quarter of an hour.

He runs off round the deck, shouting as he goes. John Harton joins Dr Jephson. He is distrait too.

HARTON: The man at the wheel says he saw nothing.

DR JEPHSON: The skylight would have blocked his view. And it's dark.

Captain Briggs is still shouting about the deck. Feet are running hither and thither, and there are shouts of sailing orders. Dr Jephson turns and goes below. Septimius Goring is inside his own cabin with his head resting on his two hands in reverie. Dr Jephson interrupts him.

DR JEPHSON: You know what's happened?
SEPTIMIUS GORING: Yes.
DR JEPHSON: Well?
SEPTIMIUS GORING: There's nothing we can do. Best get some sleep.

Dr Jephson stares at him quizzically. Septimius Goring remains in a state of immobility as the doctor closes the cabin door on him. Dr Jephson looks about the dimly-lit quarters below deck with a suggestion of premonition in his gaze. Then he turns into his own cabin. Only throwing off his jacket and loosening his collar and tie, he climbs into his bunk and, raising an arm, turns down the wick of the oil lamp. The flame gutters, and dies.
On the horizon, the first gleam of dawn is showing. Captain Briggs is standing alone in the waist of the ship staring over the grey sea. Then he turns below, leaving the empty deck behind him. For a while there is no sound except the sounds of the ship and the sea. Then another revolver shot is heard below. Dr Jephson sits up in his bed. He goes to the captain's cabin. Septimius Goring is there before him. The doctor hastily examines the body of the captain lying on the floor.

DR JEPHSON: He's dead.
SEPTIMIUS GORING: I know. He's shot himself.
DR JEPHSON (*suspiciously*): You got here very quickly.
SEPTIMUS GORING: I heard the shot.
DR JEPHSON: So did I. But I didn't get here as quickly as you did. When Mrs Briggs and her daughter fell overboard you didn't take any action at all.

SEPTIMIUS GORING: Didn't I?

> *Septimius Goring shrugs and vouchsafes the ghost of a smile. Members of the crew, black and white, gather inquisitively at the cabin entrance. Septimius Goring pushes past them. Dr Jephson stares after him. Then, after another brief examination of the dead captain, he also retires. In his cabin he is seen priming his revolver. As he does so, a maimed hand stealthily opens the cabin door. Instinctively Dr Jephson levels the weapon. Septimius Goring looks down the barrel with a bland smile.*

SEPTIMIUS GORING: You won't need that, doctor, while you have the black stone in your pocket.

> *Dr Jephson lowers the gun.*

DR JEPHSON: What do you want?

SEPTIMIUS GORING (*pressing his cheek*): Only some laudanum for the toothache.

> *The doctor reaches for the bottle in his black bag.*

DR JEPHSON (*handing the bottle over*): I shall be glad when this accursed voyage is over.

SEPTIMIUS GORING (*blandly*): According to my reckoning we're three-quarters of the way there.

DR JEPHSON: Now that we've lost the captain, your own nautical knowledge should be useful.

SEPTIMIUS GORING (*with a sinister hint in his voice*): There's still the mate to be reckoned with.

> *Dr Jephson's hand closes on his revolver again. Septimius Goring, holding the laudanum bottle, quietly closes the cabin door.*
>
> *A negro leans lazily on the ship's wheel. The first mate, scratching his cap off his head, in a state of bewilderment, is examining the compass. He seizes a chart off the deck housing, chews a pencil, and*

studies it with puzzled attention. He looks about him, as if searching for a bearing.
In the bow of the ship, John Harton is watching the spray spuming away as she dips in and out of the sea. Dr Jephson, wrapped in a muffler, joins him. The sun is just going down.

JOHN HARTON: You hardly need a muffler in this weather. The mate says that, in these latitudes, he's never known it warmer.

DR JEPHSON: The mate also says that there's a deviation in his navigating instruments he can't understand. I am glad to have this opportunity, Mr Harton, of talking to you, at any rate briefly, alone. You know, of course, that one of our white seamen has had his foot crushed by a hatch?

JOHN HARTON (*lowering his voice*): You mean it might be one of us next?

Dr Jephson coughs consumptively.

DR JEPHSON (*recovering himself*) I have a loaded revolver. We should keep together as closely as we can.

JOHN HARTON: We're off course, aren't we?

DR JEPHSON: I'm sure of it. You've travelled a lot. What's that object on the horizon out there?

JOHN HARTON (*with a low whistle*): Looks like the peak of Tenerife. But it can't be. Tenerife is five hundred miles to the south of us.

DR JEPHSON: Is that a land bird perched up there on the yard?

JOHN HARTON: Looks like a kind of chaffinch. I say, can you hear what I can? It sounds like – like the sound of surf.

As they talk, two negroes are creeping up the deck behind them. They leap on to the unsuspecting men. One of them, with the flash of a panga, brings down

*John Harton. The other, with a powerful arm
wrapped round Dr Jephson's throat, is ready to kill
him, too. A third negro – he is the cabin steward
– pulls him off. Dr Jephson reels on the deck. He
draws his pistol, but it is kicked out of his hand.*

NEGRO: Not him. The god has sent him to us with the
holy stone.

*A scream announces that another member of the crew
has been murdered. Septimius Goring appears with
a smoking pistol.*

SEPTIMIUS GORING: No more?

NEGRO: Only the white god, boss.

SEPTIMIUS GORING (*sneering*): All right, lash him up, just
to prevent him working any more miracles. Have they
signalled from the shore?

NEGRO: The war canoe is on the way, boss.

SEPTIMIUS GORING (*addressing Dr Jephson as the negroes
roughly bind his hands and legs*): You're still alive.
That's because that stone you've got is the ear of these
People's idol, stolen long ago. They believe you've been
sent from heaven to return it. If it fits, you're safe. If
it doesn't ...

He kicks him.

DR JEPHSON (*coughing*): Where are we?

SEPTIMIUS GORING: You may well ask. You're somewhere
where no white man has ever yet penetrated, the dark
country of Africa which skirts the Sahara.

*Dr Jephson stares at him, as he lies in his bonds,
through the tropical darkness. The singing and the
shouting of men drawing nearer in the war canoe
from the shore, faint at first, becomes increasingly
closer.*

DR JEPHSON: But why? I know now, I knew before,

that you murdered the captain and his family and . . .
Is John Harton dead?

SEPTIMIUS GORING (*viciously*): All the white men, except
you are dead.

DR JEPHSON (*weakly*) : You arranged the deviations in the
navigating instruments. You must have planned this for
a very long time?

SEPTIMIUS GORING (*emotionally*): All my life. I lost my
fingers, these, when I was tortured by a white boss.
I was a slave, you understand, I've fought through my
life. . . .

DR JEPHSON: You mean murdered.

SEPTIMIUS GORING: We've got a lot to catch up on the
white man.

DR JEPHSON: And now?

SEPTIMIUS GORING (*raising his hands and his eyes to the
sky*): Uhuru! (*coming down to earth again*) I couldn't
have expected that you would be a competitor.

> *The noise of the exuberant men in the approaching
> war canoe is now overwhelming. Two of the negroes,
> on a signal from Septimius Goring, gather up Dr
> Jephson, and bundle him off.*
> *The black stone in Dr Jephson's pocket saved his life.
> It fitted the idol like a lost piece in a jigsaw puzzle.
> The black people thought that he must be a divine
> person to bring it back to them. Septimius Goring
> had to procure his escape to establish his own dic-
> tatorship. He cast Dr Jephson away on a native boat
> from which he was subsequently picked up by a
> passing steamer.*

Before long, the story appeared as the true account of
what had happened aboard *Mary Celeste* in American
newspapers. It was now eleven years since she had been
brought a derelict into Gibraltar Harbour, a mere year
before she broke up on a Haitian reef.

Now in his seventies, Mr Solly Flood registered his

irascible, irrepressible, indefatigable protest at what he called a travesty of truth.

John Dickson Carr, Conan Doyle's biographer, tells how the story 'had repercussions beyond mere critical praise... Through the medium of the Central News Agency, a telegram was thrown back widespread over England:

'MR SOLLY FLOOD, HER MAJESTY'S ADVOCATE GENERAL AT GIBRALTAR, PRONOUNCES DR J. HABAKUK JEPHSON'S STATEMENT A FABRICATION FROM BEGINNING TO END.

'Mr Flood also wrote a long report to his Government and to the newspapers, pointing out the menace to international relations when people like this Dr Jephson professed to reveal facts which on many points could be officially disproved.'

Consul Horatio Sprague, also still functioning, was moved to write to the Assistant Secretary of State in Washington, suggesting a cross-examination of the author of what he described as 'romance of a very unlikely and exaggerated nature.'

> '*Honorable John Davis,*
> *Asst Secretary of State, Washington.*
> *Sir, My attention has been called to an article which appears in the Cornhill Magazine for this month, entitled '*J. Habakuk Jephson's Statement*' in which is referred the American brigantine* Mary Celeste *of New York, which was met at sea on the 4th December 1872 in latitude 38° 20' longitude 17° 15' W by the British brigantine* Dei Gratia, *and brought into this port as a derelict, the full particulars of which were at the time duly transmitted to the department.*
> '*It having ever since remained a mystery regarding the fate of the master and crew of the* Mary Celeste, *or even the cause that induced or forced them to abandon the vessel which, with her cargo, were found when met by the* Dei Gratia *to be in perfect order, I ask (*sic*) to myself,*

what motives can have prompted the writer of the article in question to refer to this mysterious affair, after the lapse of eleven years; especially as the statement given is not only replete with inaccuracies as regards the date, voyage and destination of the vessel, names of the parties constituting her crew, and the fact of her having no passengers on board beyond the master's wife and child, but seems to me to be replete with romance of a very unlikely or exaggerated nature.

'As the Department cannot fail to feel a certain interest to ascertain whether there be the least suspicion of truth in any porion of what is stated in the article referred to in the Cornhill Magazine, I have taken the liberty to call its attention to it, especially as it may have the opportunity of examining the author of this extraordinary composition.

'With reference to the crew of Mary Celeste, I beg to enclose herewith a list of their names, according to her clearance for Genoa at the New York Custom house; also copy of a communication I received in 1873 from Prussia, referring to two of the crew, represented as being brothers, and evidently of German extraction.

'I am, Sir, Your obedient Servant,
Horatio H. Sprague, U.S. Consul, Gibraltar.'

The reply to Mr Sprague from Mr John Davis, the Assistant Secretary of State was formal and non-committal.

'The article to which you refer has been read with attention and much interest. The mystery which surrounds the fate of the master and crew and the passengers, or even the cause that induced or forced them to abandon their vessel, is in no wise satisfactorily explained in that statement, and it is conceived that, from the information we now possess, no solution of the mystery has yet been presented.

'Under the circumstances, the Department has not deemed it essential to pursue any particular enquiries into

the antecedents of the writer of the article in question, leaving the matter to a further development of the facts which time alone may or will develop....'

Officialdom in London and Washington made a humourless note on the matter. The doctor who perpetrated the story had no cause to do anything about it. Yet, just as it was he who conceived the prototype detectives have modelled themselves on ever since, it was he also who started the trail of people who claimed to be survivors of *Mary Celeste*.

7. THE SCHOOL SERVANT'S STORY

In 1913, the *Strand Magazine*, then at the height of its influence with a large international circulation, invited some of the most eminent storytellers of the day to suggest their own solution of 'the most famous mystery of the sea'. They included, besides Sir Arthur Conan Doyle, who had been knighted in 1902, the inventions of writers such as Arthur Morrison, Barry Pain, Morley Roberts and Horace Annesley Vachell. Readers were asked to join in. The invitation to the *Strand*'s readers led to 'an important announcement'; the discovery of what appeared to be, in the editor's words, 'a perfectly genuine account of the disaster left by a survivor'.

In the issue of October, 1913, the *Strand* promised a sensational development. In the next number, above the traditional woodcut on the frontispiece of the street scene in the Strand, Conan Doyle's new story, 'The Horror of the Heights' was given second box. Bannered over the title of the magazine was 'AMAZING SOLUTION OF THE MYSTERY OF MARIE CELESTE'....

In reply to the invitation to suggest an answer Mr Howard Linford M.A., of Magdalen, Oxford, headmaster of Hampstead's largest preparatory school, disclosed that he had discovered a manuscript among the posthumous effects of an elderly school servant named Abel Fosdyk. There was no question of Mr Linford's repute and responsibility. As the *Strand* authoritatively stated: '*Mr A. Howard Linford, the headmaster of Peterborough Lodge, is well known in the scholastic world as a man who has fought hard for the better teaching of mathematics and*

*English to the young as being the essentials of a scientific
training. He has met his just reward by the success of his
pupils in the public schools.'*

There was more to the same effect. None could doubt
the veracity of a headmaster, and an M.A. to boot. Further, he told that his son, then a schoolboy at Harrow,
had made sketches under the old man's direction. With
some artistic gift, the boy had made a record of what
happened. The editor of the *Strand* used the pencilled
notes to get one of his top artists to illustrate it.

It looked as if the magazine which had scooped the
world with the exclusive story of Captain Scott's fatal
expedition to the South Pole had done it again. I can
imagi : the excitement in Tower House, Southampton
Street, when the November, 1913, number went to press.
Forty years later I was to edit the magazine myself. But
I would have been more careful of my facts. When the
Strand first flew the kite it is evident that nobody in the
office had checked details which were readily available
in Gibraltar. Captain Briggs was described as 'Captain
Griggs'. Morehouse, the master of the *Dei Gratia*, was
nam d as 'Boyce'. It seems that when Mr Linford appeared on the scene some attempt was made to correct the
record. Writing to the editor, Mr Linford shows a peda-
gogue's regard for exactness:

*'Sir – A friend has brought to my notice your article
on the Marie Celeste. When I read it the name struck
a familiar chord, but it was some days before I could
remember under what circumstances I had heard it. At
last, however, I recalled an old servant, Abel Fosdyk,
committing to my charge, on his deathbed, a quantity of
papers contained in three boxes; amongst these he told
me would be found the account of (the) Mary Celeste. I
suppose he said "the", but I had at the time no notion of
what Mary Celeste meant, and imagined it was a woman.
I paid but little heed, and merely sent the boxes away
to a safe keeping, not anticipating that they would ever*

be opened again. Before commenting on the matter I would like to emphasize the fact that I do not vouch for the truth of anything narrated. No word on the subject was ever mentioned by the writer to me. But the fact that for thirty years he kept not only a diary but also a set of shrewd observations on all that passed, and wrote much and well without our knowing anything of what he was doing, shows him to have been a man of exceptional reticence and self-control.

'*As for the document, I would rather let it speak for itself; but at the same time I must confess that I have been greatly impressed by the following facts: A brig called Marie Celeste, sailing under a Captain Griggs. By your courtesy I have now seen the official report, and find in every instance the papers in my possession are correct. Further, the official papers mention a peculiar damage to the bows and two square cuts on the outside. This, I think, has never till now been made public, yet there again the papers I send you enter most minutely into this alteration of the bows. Finally I find, on enquiry, that the autumn of 1872 was famous for its extraordinary storms in the Atlantic, so much so that a leading article in the Times likens it to the period of storms so well known to have prevailed at Cromwell's death. One can easily imagine a captain, working day and night in such conditions, going gradually out of his mind.*

'*Of course, minute errors will always creep in when relating facts a long time after their occurrence. It is evident to me these facts were written down nearly twenty years after they happened, and no one knows better than myself how easily dates may be forgotten or the sequence of events confused.*

'*I now leave the M.S. in your hands.*'

I suspect that Mr Linford's letter was not his original one to the editor. It looks to me like a letter contrived when publication was determined. Abel Fosdyk, in one of his boxes, left a photograph of a little girl, wrapped in a

piece of paper, on which he wrote the words in pencil,
'Baby at the age of two years'. The *Strand* reproduced
it. It also published a facsimile of a portion of Abel
Fosdyk's manuscript.

In my own version, this is the story that he told, which
the then editor of the *Strand* described as 'so vivid and
so alive, so simple and yet so unlikely to be thought of,
that one seems to hear the ring of truth in every word'.
Well....

> *Under storm canvas, Mary Celeste is riding a gale.
> Captain Briggs, in foul weather clothes, is at the
> wheel. He is capless, with an unkempt beard and
> bedraggled hair. The way he hangs on the spokes of
> the wheel shows his weariness. His eyes have a wild
> gleam in them. In this version, he is stark staring
> mad. The chief mate struggles over the narrow strip
> of deck past the after deckhouse on to the poop.*

MATE (*cupping his hands to shout into the captain's ear
over the gale*): Tops'l and fors'l gone, sir.
CAPTAIN BRIGGS: I've got eyes. Bend the storm fore and
aft mains'l ready for setting.
MATE: Aye, aye, sir.
He picks up a speaking trumpet.
MATE: Bend the fore and aft mains'l.

> *Two hands scale the mainmast ratlines to the yards.
> As the vessel swings drunkenly in the seas, they hang
> on to the yards, clearing with freezing hands the
> tattered sails. At the end of a yard, one of the men
> loses his hold. He tumbles, with a lost scream, into
> the sea.*

MATE: Man overboard.
CAPTAIN BRIGGS (*spinning the wheel*): I'm heaving to.
You can swim. Pick him up.
MATE: In this weather?
CAPTAIN BRIGGS: You can swim.

MATE: Not in a sea like this.

CAPTAIN BRIGGS: You heard my orders.

MATE: I've got heavy clothes on, sir, I can't help him. If I go over the side, I'll drown, too. We can't even risk launching the ship's boat. For all our sakes....

He looks over the raging sea, and crosses himself.

MATE: He was a good man, too.

CAPTAIN BRIGGS: You're a coward.

MATE: With respect, sir. I think no one need feel ashamed of refusing to go into a sea like this. One's enough. I'll see to the canvas.

Going forward, the mate scales into the rigging himself. Captain Briggs glowers over the wheel. A sail opens into the wind. The mate slides down a rope on to the dripping deck. Coming aft, he again addresses his captain.

MATE: Storm canvas set, sir.

CAPTAIN BRIGGS: I can see that.

MATE: He was one of our best seamen. But there was nothing we could do to help him in this, sir.

The mate hesitates.

CAPTAIN BRIGGS: Well, what are you waiting for?

MATE: I was thinking that in all my experience of the sea, I've never known four weeks of weather like this.

CAPTAIN BRIGGS: That's not what you want to say. Come on, out with it.

MATE: You've been driving yourself too hard, sir. It's not often that the skipper takes as many tricks at the wheel as you have.

CAPTAIN BRIGGS: What else can I do with a crew of cowards aboard.

MATE: With respect, sir.

CAPTAIN BRIGGS (*sneering*): You had heavy clothes on ...

MATE: You ought to go below, sir, for a rest. Your wife's poorly.

CAPTAIN BRIGGS: And leave you to let the *Celeste* go to the bottom – because you've got your clothes on?

MATE: I think the weather's moderating. If you'll only rest for a while ... we've got a good crew, sir.

CAPTAIN BRIGGS: Thirteen of them.

MATE: No, sir, fourteen now. With Smith, we were fifteen.

CAPTAIN BRIGGS: If I hear any more nonsense about thirteen being an unlucky number, I'll knock your head off. And then we'll be twelve, won't we?

MATE: No, fourteen.

CAPTAIN BRIGGS: Are you suggesting that I don't know the number of my own ship's company?

MATE: With respect, sir.

CAPTAIN BRIGGS: A fine chief mate I've got. Won't go into the water with his clothes on.

MATE: If you'll let me have the wheel, Mrs Briggs is anxious to see you, sir.

CAPTAIN BRIGGS (*slyly*): And you're anxious to see the back of me, aren't you? You think I'm not fit to command this ship? Answer!

Captain Briggs relaxes his hold on the wheel and, sitting on the skylight, begins to sob. The mate, soberly, takes over. After a while, the captain staggers to his feet, and goes below; leaving the mate in charge. Below Captain Briggs reels into the Captain's cabin. His daughter is playing with her toys. His wife is lying on the bed.

On his entrance, Mrs Briggs, pale with seasickness, gets to her feet, and tries to comfort him. Pushing her aside, he begins throwing off his clothes. Sensing the atmosphere, the child slips out of the cabin. She is seven or eight years old in this version – sturdy, square-built and short, with reddish hair, and dressed in a dark blue jersey and frock, with short socks. She climbs the companionway and, half opening the sliding door of the deckhouse, looks out mischievously over the rolling sea washed ship.

The mate is standing steadily at the wheel, watching the set of the sails. A man with a billycan of tea reels aft from the galley in the forward deckhouse. He is Abel Fosdyk, the steward. He joins the mate at the wheel.

FOSDYK: What you need is a drop of tea.

MATE: You're right, I do.

FOSDYK: Sticky weather.

He passes the billycan. The mate takes a gulp of the liquid. Then his hand drops. Abel Fosdyk follows his eyes. Captain Briggs' daughter is making her way across the maindeck. As they look at her she slips and falls.

MATE: Call a seaman to take the wheel, Fosdyk; and you report to the captain.

He reaches the child and lifts her, not without effort, as he holds on to the standing rigging, to her feet.

BABY: I'm all right.

MATE (*breathing heavily with the effort*): You might have gone overboard. What would your Papa have said then?

BABY: He's asleep now.

MATE: Come on, I'll help you below.

BABY: I don't want to stay below. I've been there all the time.

MATE: You come with me.

With rough affection, the mate guides her to the entrance of the after deckhouse as Captain Briggs,

The School Servant's Story

half-dressed and wild-eyed, with no eyes for his daughter, explodes on to the deck.

CAPTAIN BRIGGS (*to the mate*): What's going on? The moment I leave, you all seem to go mad.

MATE: I don't think so, sir.

CAPTAIN BRIGGS: The steward says you've thrown my daughter overboard.

MATE: She's safe, sir.

CAPTAIN BRIGGS: That's not what the steward said.

MATE: Abel Fosdyk, I'm sure, sir, reported to you that your daughter was on deck. But she's safe now.

Abel Fosdyk, the steward, reappears with another can of tea.

FOSDYK: What you need, skipper, is a drop of tea.

Captain Briggs seems to welcome it. Then, suddenly, he knocks the billycan out of Fosdyk's hands. He is staring forrard, with mouth open and eyes burning out of his head. His daughter is balancing herself, with free hands, on the bowsprit of the ship.

CAPTAIN BRIGGS: Good God, look there! It's Baby!

Fosdyk, also barefooted, sprints over the deck to the bows.

FOSDYK (*addressing the little girl as calmly as he can*): Darling, you mustn't go there. You might fall in.

BABY: I've often done it before; and nobody said I mustn't.

FOSDYK: Well, darling, it's like this. Papa's not well, and it frightens him; and you wouldn't want to do that, would you?

BABY: No.

The little girl jumps into Fosdyk's arms as Captain Briggs appears.

CAPTAIN BRIGGS (*to the child*): Like everybody else on this ship, you're disobeying my orders.

He boxes her ears. He sends her, crying below. He swings on Abel Fosdyk.

CAPTAIN BRIGGS: You're the steward on this ship, responsible for everybody below. Like all the rest of the crew – I've got a coward for a mate – you're willing to let my own daughter drown to save yourselves work. What's your name?

FOSDYK: Abel Fosdyk, sir.

CAPTAIN BRIGGS: Probably a false name to keep you out of prison. Very well, Mr Fosdyk – one of the thirteen of you on this ship – order the carpenter, with my compliments, to make a safe berth on this bowsprit for my daughter. He can lash on an upturned table, make a rail, where she can have her own quarter deck. Understood?

FOSDYK (*puzzled*): Understood, sir.

CAPTAIN BRIGGS: You say that as if you think I'm mad.

FOSDYK: No, sir. Certainly not, sir.

CAPTAIN BRIGGS: You, you're too tall for a small ship like this.

FOSDYK: I'm very comfortable, sir.

CAPTAIN BRIGGS: I'll make you very uncomfortable if you don't obey my orders.

FOSDYK: Yes, sir.

CAPTAIN BRIGGS: What were my orders?

FOSDYK: Build a quarter deck here on the bowsprit for the Baby, sir.

CAPTAIN BRIGGS: Then, don't stand there arguing, get on with it.

Abel Fosdyk, relieved to be released, patters aft. Mrs Briggs comes forrard and, although she is plainly under the weather, puts her arm around her husband's shoulder.

Captain Benjamin Spooner Briggs, a studio portrait taken more than a hundred years ago, as he looked when he sailed on his fatal voyage in *Mary Celeste*

Mrs Briggs, the master's wife who disappeared with him, with her son Arthur Stanley Briggs who was left behind in New England to continue his schooling

Albert Richardson, first mate of *Mary Celeste*. To the end of her life his widow was convinced that the officers were the victims of mutiny and murder

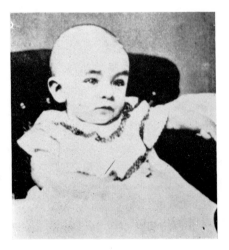

Sophia Matilda Briggs, the two-year-old daughter of Captain and Mrs Briggs, who was lost with them at sea. There is no question as to the authenticity of the tired old photographs

Captain David Reed
Morehouse, master
of the *Dei Gratia*,
from a photograph
taken in Gibraltar
about 1873

Oliver Deveau, first
mate of the *Dei
Gratia* who, with
only two other
seamen, brought
Mary Celeste into
Gibraltar in
December 1872. The
British authorities
believed that all three
men were liars

In 1913 the *Strand
Magazine*, then at the
height of its influence
with a large inter-
national circulation,
believed the claim of
a preparatory school-
master of undoubted
propriety who said that
he had had a servant,
named Abel Fosdyk,
whose posthumous pap
told the true story of
Mary Celeste. Fosdyk
was supposed to have
been aboard her

The schoolmaster reported an extraordinary account of how Captain Briggs went mad, and his whole crew fell overboard from a temporary platform made for the master's daughter on her bowsprit. Convinced that the story was true, the *Strand* commissioned one of their top illustrators to reconstruct it. Here is what was published as the scoop to settle the mystery

The Rock of Gibraltar approximately at the time when *Mary Celeste* was brought a derelict into the harbour. In the engraving it looks barely inhabited. In fact it hummed with life and gossip

THE MOST IMPUDENT IMPOSTURE: a Liverpool Irish journalist half-fooled the world with his book *The Great Mary Celeste Hoax*. His publishers, who no longer exist, thought that they were on to a good thing, and publicised it accordingly. Nothing in this has the least resemblance to truth. Yet it is absurd but true that many believed that this was the answer

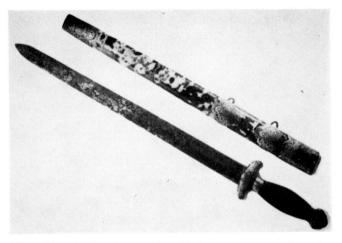

The 'bloodstained' sword which was supposed to be evidence of mutiny and murder. Fourteen years after, it was shown that information which had been suppressed proved that the accusation had no validity

The melodeon which Mrs Briggs introduced into the cabin. It is still preserved by a descendant of the family in New England. It played a part in one of the impostors' stories

MRS BRIGGS: You frightened Baby.

CAPTAIN BRIGGS: Baby frightened me. You know what she did.

MRS BRIGGS: Yes, yes. I know. But you shouldn't make her cry.

CAPTAIN BRIGGS: She made me cry.

MRS BRIGGS: A man should keep his head.

CAPTAIN BRIGGS: Keep his head. Do you realize we've got a chief mate who's a coward? He wouldn't go into the sea with his clothes on?

MRS BRIGGS: Let's go below, dear. I'm sure that, if you have some of the sleep you've lost, you'll feel better. You haven't got to worry about the weather now. At last, the sea is calmer.

Mrs Briggs offers her arm to her husband who, not unwillingly, allows her to lead him below. Captain Briggs, his wife and daughter lie on the bunk in the Captain's cabin. The crew sleeps too. The morning rises on a calm sea, with the man at the wheel handling the ship with a lazy single hand. Abel Fosdyk bustles aft with the tea.

FOSDYK (*passing the billycan*): All quiet in the captain's cabin. All's well in a quiet sea.

SEAMAN: Captain Briggs is off his head, isn't he?

FOSDYK: Captains never go off their heads, not like the rest of us.

SEAMAN: Still, you know what I mean.

FOSDYK: We needn't worry about Baby any more.

SEAMAN: You mean now she's got her own quarterdeck.

Above the bowsprit of the ship, a rigging has been fixed out of an upturned table with a rail.

FOSDYK: Look. . . .

Baby trips out of the after-cabin, and climbs delightedly into the contraption. She seats herself on a small barrel which has been placed in the corner.

F   81

Fosdyk, with a smile, goes forrard past the smoking galley chimney.

FOSDYK: Happy now?

Baby rises to her feet and, holding her hand over her eyes, calls:

BABY: Ship on the port bow!

She looks at Fosdyk.

BABY: When are you going to tell me the story of Ali Baba and the Forty Thieves again?

FOSDYK: As soon as I've served breakfast.

BABY: Can I come with you?

FOSDYK: Of course, darling.

He lifts her down. She looks over her shoulder.

BABY (*happily*): I like having my own quarterdeck.

FOSDYK: You're safe there.

Hand in hand they go to the galley where a saucepan of porridge is boiling on the iron stove. Fosdyk busies himself completing the loading of a tray for the saloon.

BABY: Can I carry something?

FOSDYK: If you're careful.

BABY: The deck isn't at all slippery.

Baby, with a loaf of bread under her arm, and Abel Fosdyk carrying a tray of porridge, bacon and tea go aft to the saloon. Captain Briggs, resting his chin morosely on his hands, is waiting at the table with his wife and the mate.

MRS BRIGGS: Something to cheer you up, dear. Here's Abel with Baby – and the breakfast.

Captain Briggs shows no interest as Abel Fosdyk arranges the table, and serves the food. Abel Fosdyk remains present, popping in and out of the pantry.

CAPTAIN BRIGGS: I can't put it out of my mind. I've been dreaming about it all night. A man who says that he can't swim with his clothes on.

MATE: I agree sir, that you can keep afloat, and move a bit, but you can't do much; not really to call it swimming, that is.

CAPTAIN BRIGGS: A man can't swim in his clothes, hey?

MATE: Not an ordinary man can't. You mustn't judge by yourself. There aren't many who can swim like you.

CAPTAIN BRIGGS: At school, I won three swimming prizes three years running. You know that?

MATE: You've mentioned it, sir.

MRS BRIGGS: You haven't stopped talking about it for days, dear.

CAPTAIN BRIGGS: Why not?

Mrs Briggs, trying to change the subject, attends to Baby, who is watching her father with wide-eyed attention.

MRS BRIGGS (*to Baby*): Now get on with your breakfast, there's a dear. You haven't been eating enough lately. Is there enough sugar on the porridge? Is it too hot?

CAPTAIN BRIGGS: A man can't swim with his clothes on.

MRS BRIGGS: Never mind about that. Just have your breakfast.

CAPTAIN BRIGGS (*slowly and abstractedly*): I'm not going to have my breakfast now.

He pushes aside his plate.

MRS BRIGGS: Not going to have your breakfast. Stuff and nonsense.

CAPTAIN BRIGGS: I'm not going to have my breakfast yet.

MRS BRIGGS: And why not, pray?

CAPTAIN BRIGGS: I'm going to have a swim in my clothes.

MRS BRIGGS: You're not. Don't you think it.

CAPTAIN BRIGGS (*rising to his feet*): We shall see about that.

MATE: What are you taking on so about, sir? I didn't mean you. We all know that you can do anything in the water.

CAPTAIN BRIGGS (*moving towards the companionway*): That'll do, that'll do.

MRS BRIGGS: You don't mean it, dear.

Mrs Briggs is on the edge of tears.

CAPTAIN BRIGGS: Of course I mean it. I can swim in my clothes.

MATE (*hurriedly*): But you've got good clothes, sir. What's the sense in spoiling them? They're not like these slops of mine.

CAPTAIN BRIGGS: Very well, we'll change clothes; and I'll give you a new suit if I don't get round the ship in five minutes. That's fair, isn't it?

MATE: I think it's a great pity you're even thinking of such a thing.

CAPTAIN BRIGGS: You would; you who say a man can't swim with his clothes on.

MRS BRIGGS (*to mate*): If he won't stop for me, he won't stop for you.

CAPTAIN BRIGGS: If there's any more nonsense about it, I shall take Baby on my back, and we'll both go.

Captain Briggs throws off his coat and waistcoat on to the locker. Mrs Briggs sobs into her handkerchief. With a look of unbelief, the mate takes off his watch and chain, and puts them on the table. Then he himself slowly unbuttons his own waistcoat.

MRS BRIGGS: No, no.

CAPTAIN BRIGGS: Nothing to worry about. A dip in the sea is just the very thing to brace me up and put me all right. I've been feeling seedy. I'll show you whether a man can swim in his clothes, or not. (*to the mate*) Come with me.

With a fractional shrug of his shoulders, the mate follows him out of the cabin. Mrs Briggs, sniffing in her handkerchief, glances at Abel Fosdyk.

MRS BRIGGS: Can you swim, Abel?

ABEL FOSDYK: Not very good with my clothes on, ma'am.

MRS BRIGGS: My husband isn't well. He might get cramp or anything.

ABEL FOSDYK: He's a good swimmer, and it's as calm as a millpool now. He'll be all right.

MRS BRIGGS: Why does he have to do it?

ABEL FOSDYK (*tidying things on the table*): I think the heavy weather's upset him, ma'am. I call him one of the best masters I've ever sailed under.

MRS BRIGGS (*getting to her feet*): Thank you for that, Abel. Come on, Baby, we'll watch Daddy swim round the ship.

Hand in hand, the two of them leave the cabin. Fiddling for a few moments with the uneaten breakfast, glancing apprehensively up the companionway, Abel Fosdyk follows them. On deck, in the mate's slops, Captain Briggs is waiting to go over the side. Two other men are stripped down to their pants to join him. Mrs Briggs, holding Baby's hand, is on 'Baby's Quarterdeck'. The other members of the crew are forrard, too. Captain Briggs levers himself over the side, and hangs on a knotted rope by the jib boom chains.

CAPTAIN BRIGGS: I'll go when Baby gives me the order 'Go'.

BABY (*leaning over the side*): Go!

Captain Briggs drops into the water. Two other men dive after him. The rest, including Mrs Briggs, hang over 'Baby's Quarterdeck', watching with the other men immediately behind him.

ABEL FOSDYK: He's round the stern! He's all right, Mrs
Briggs!

*The crew who have been leaning over the starboard
side, change excitedly to the port. 'Baby's Quarterdeck' groans under their weight, and slips. They are
all tumbled into the sea. The platform, its lashings
broken, dangles by one of its ends to the bowsprit,
with only one member of the crew hanging on. Abel
Fosdyk surfaces, and swims towards the survivor.*

ABEL FOSDYK (*gasping*): What's happened?
SEAMAN: Look after yourself. There's a shark after us.

*The fin of a shark shows in the water. Captain Briggs
is seen struggling in the sea, and bloodily disappear-
ing. Abel Fosdyk grabs the 'Baby's Quarterdeck'
while he hangs over the side. With the extra weight,
it breaks away. The second man looses his grip.
Another clutches on to it, and crawls aboard Abel
Fosdyk follows him. The man already aboard rolls
off dead. Abel Fosdyk clings on. He watches the* Mary
Celeste, *her wheel unguarded, sail into the distance.
Abel Fosdyk rides alone on 'Baby's Quarterdeck'.*

It was a good story for an elderly school servant, once
of the sea. It explained, as Conan Doyle conjectured, how
a vessel could be found abandoned with all her ship's
boats intact. It supported the myth of a half-finished
breakfast. It offered a solution of the strange marks on
the ship's bows. What Abel Fosdyk didn't explain was
how a baby of two became a child of seven. The story
is incredible.

The single ship's boat, when she was found, had been
launched. There was no half-finished breakfast unless the
Dei Gratia's crew told less than they knew. There is no
official record that Abel Fosdyk was ever a member of
Mary Celeste's crew. It seems to me possible that he might
have been one of those people, more common than many

suspect, with a compulsive imagination; although I find it surprising that a man of his sort could have invented his tale. The account of the background facts of the case – the three seaman's trunks, the death bed manuscript, the photograph – contains all the simpler tricks of fiction. I look elsewhere. It is surprising what men will presume, even scholars, for a handful of sovereigns.

8. CAPTAIN LUCY'S STORY

On September 24, 1924, London's *Daily Express* headlined a scoop:

GREAT SEA MYSTERY CLEARED UP.
What happened to the *Mary Celeste*.
Derelict Gold: Crew's Escape with Stolen £3,500.

After more than fifty years, it was nice to think that here was the truth of the matter. The *Daily Express* had found a beached sea captain, Captain R. Lucy, R.N.R; a man respected, the newspaper reported, all over the Mediterranean and in Eastern waters, who claimed that he was the only man living who knew how the *Mary Celeste* was abandoned. He learnt the facts, he said, forty-two years before. He now believed himself free, at the age of seventy, to speak. Captain Lucy, wounded in the Dardanelles, awarded the Croix de Guerre and the Italian Cross of Merit, told that he heard the true story of the *Mary Celeste* when he was mate of the *Island Princess*, cruising in the South Seas. It was told to him under oath (there is always an oath involved) by a man called Triggs, whom he had met in the Bay View Hotel, Melbourne. He subsequently found a job for him as 'bos'n of our Kanaka crew'. 'Triggs, though I am sure it was an assumed name, had been bos'n of the *Mary Celeste*. I only learnt it after living in the same ship with him for three months. But, bit by bit, he told me his story.' Here is Triggs' version:

Captain Briggs is at his desk in his cabin, chewing a cigar. In this tale, he is a sort of American 'Captain Morgan'. Triggs, another piratical character, reports to him. By way of introduction, he throws himself on a seat.

CAPTAIN BRIGGS: Want something?

Captain Briggs fills an empty glass with a dram of rum.

TRIGGS (*helping himself to a drink*): We've sighted a steamer to starboard.

CAPTAIN BRIGGS: Has she spoken us?

TRIGGS: She isn't steaming. She's rolling about like a dead duck. We think she's a derelict.

He gulps his drink.

TRIGGS: Thought you might like to have a look at her. Might be something useful aboard.

CAPTAIN BRIGGS: Unlike this tub?

TRIGGS: We're willing to have a go.

Captain Briggs empties his glass and, picking up binoculars, rolls on to the deck. He is followed by Triggs, and joined by the mate and another disreputable-looking seaman.

MATE: Looks like a prize, skipper.

Captain Briggs raises his glass. Through the lenses, a rusty-looking ship is rolling in the sea.

TRIGGS: There ought to be something worth lifting aboard her.

CAPTAIN BRIGG: You'll probably need grappling irons, and ropes.

It was evident, Captain Lucy explained, what the discovery of a derelict like that meant to a miserable little sailing tramp running out from New York to Genoa with a cargo of rubbish.

The sea was calm. Triggs, the mate and four others, rowed across to the steamer. The action of the seawater had rusted her, and washed her name away. All that they could discern was that she was registered in London. But, in the purser's cabin, they found an iron safe. They returned excitedly to *Mary Celeste* for carpenter's tools to burst open the door. The safe contained three thousand five hundred pounds in gold and silver.

'You will appreciate,' said Captain Lucy, 'what that meant to men like them. They had to launch three of the ship's boats left on the derelict ship to carry the coin back to the *Mary Celeste*. Before he left the steamer Captain Briggs, who had come aboard, gave orders to the carpenter to go below and open out one of the watercocks, and sink her, as she might be a danger to shipping. Then, with the load of gold, the crew returned to the *Celeste*.

In the saloon of Mary Celeste, *Triggs, the mate and members of the crew empty bags of coin on the table. It spills all over the place, as treasure should. The men scrabble for it delightedly.*

CAPTAIN BRIGGS: You do the counting, Triggs. We can trust you.

Triggs builds the coin in piles as the others talk.

MATE: How are we going to divide the spoils?
CAPTAIN BRIGGS: There's an unwritten rule of the sea that the captain takes one-third. My suggestion is that the mate should have one-fifth, the bos'n one-eighth, and the rest divided among the rest of the crew.
MATE: What about your wife and child?
CAPTAIN BRIGGS (*grinning*): We can regard them as cargo. They don't count for a share.
TRIGGS (*piling up money*): Are you sure what we're doing is legal? Under marine law it's an offence, isn't it, to lift money like this?
MATE: We're not pirates. She was deserted.
CAPTAIN BRIGGS: Triggs has a point all the same. We can

all do with the money; but I fancy they'll call it Treasure Trove, or something. We might lose the lot.

They all look at Captain Briggs in dismay.

CAPTAIN BRIGGS: They might suggest that we didn't come by it honestly. We might be called upon to prove that she was a derelict ship.

MATE: Not much we could say now, now she's at the bottom.

CAPTAIN BRIGGS: We don't even know her name.

The money is piling on the table; but the crew are looking questioningly, not at the gold, but at Captain Briggs.

CAPTAIN BRIGGS (*pulling a chart towards him*): My reckoning is that we ought to pick up the coast of Spain or Portugal in the next twenty-four hours. In the ship's boats from the steamer, we could make Cadiz.

TRIGGS: And sink the *Mary Celeste*?

Captain Briggs nods. Triggs completes his calculation.

TRIGGS: Three thousand five hundred.

CAPTAIN BRIGGS: That shouldn't be difficult to divide.

He makes a calculation on a scrap of paper. They all watch him anxiously.

CAPTAIN BRIGGS: My suggestion is twelve hundred for the captain's share. The mate six hundred, the second mate four hundred, Triggs the bos'un three hundred, and the remainder equally divided among the crew. Satisfied?

MATE: Sounds fair to me.

TRIGGS: And me.

A seaman enters the cabin.

CAPTAIN BRIGGS: Well?

SEAMAN: Ship speaking us.
CAPTAIN BRIGGS: Have you answered her?
SEAMAN: Yes.
CAPTAIN BRIGGS: Leave it at that.

The seaman, with a wide-eyed look at the gold, returns.

CAPTAIN BRIGGS: You realize what that means. Now we've been sighted, we can't sink the brig. Foul play will be suspected. If we want to get away with it, we've got to do better than that.
TRIGGS: Can't we still run in to Genoa?
CAPTAIN BRIGGS: Where you'll all get drunk on the money – and talk. No, we've got to do better than that. Somehow, I've got to lose the *Mary Celeste* – and good riddance – and lose ourselves as well.
TRIGGS: We could man the ship's boats off the steamer. When we come in, they won't know where we come from.
CAPTAIN BRIGGS: You've got it, Triggs! Call all hands. We'll abandon ship!

Captain Briggs leads the rush from the cabin.

TRIGGS: Captain's orders. Abandon ship!

Captain Lucy's story ended that they painted the three boats from the derelict steamer with the name of a schooner belonging to London, and loaded themselves aboard, with the money, food and water. They arrived safely in Cadiz early the following day, and reported the loss of the schooner whose name they had painted on their boats. They said that she had struck a submerged wreck. Triggs went on to Australia. He never saw any of his shipmates again. 'That's it,' ended Captain Lucy, 'the story that was told to me more than forty years ago. It has often made me smile to read the elaborate solutions attempted in many ports of the world to explain the mystery of the *Mary Celeste*.'

If Bos'n Triggs' story about *Mary Celeste* was the true one, Captain Lucy had good cause to smile. Presumably, the *Daily Express* paid him well for his information. In the context of this book, Triggs' account of the matter doesn't make much sense. Why should Captain Briggs decide to abandon his ship, of which he was part owner, for a sum of money far less than his own ship was worth to him, even if her cargo (which it wasn't) was rubbish.

What is remarkable is that Triggs' story was widely believed, and reprinted as the final solution. Conan Doyle's imaginative story had been accepted by the *Boston Herald* as fact. Abel Fosdyk's story, published with the authority of the *Strand Magazine*, backed by the evidence of a preparatory schoolmaster, none less, seemed to settle the matter. Readers were fooled by the magic of print. It is probable that, even now, only a small minority disbelieves what they read in the papers, or look at on TV.

The story of *Mary Celeste* is the more important because it is an example of what people will believe; and what others, for their own gain, will kid themselves into believing. *Mary Celeste* is a test of truth. Yet, examining the case, I am inclined to think that most people don't want truth. It is far more exciting, in a dull existence, to adventure into the realms of romance.

I am a hunter of truth. But I am also a writer of fiction. So I have a certain respect for the man who pulled off the most astonishing story of what happened.

9. KEATING'S HOAX

In 1929, more than half a century after any sort of solution of the mystery might have seemed possible, an article appeared in *Chambers' Journal* which seemed to explain the whole business. Its author signed himself Lee Kaye. The substance of what he wrote was reprinted about the world.

It was no story this time about a man long dead. It seemed that there was still an elderly man living in Liverpool who knew all about it. He had been aboard *Mary Celeste* on her fateful voyage. His name was John Pemberton.

Two years later, there could have hardly have been more solid confirmation that this wasn't another story of an old man of the sea than the appearance of a book called *The Great Mary Celeste Hoax*. The author was a man named Laurence J. Keating, clearly the same man who had written in *Chambers' Journal* under the pseudonym of 'Lee Kaye'. Nothing wrong in that. When the book was published, reviewers in Britain and America were convinced that here, so many years later, was the truth at last.

All the newspapers sought out John Pemberton for an interview. He proved evasive. But, in the end, the London *Evening Standard* got an exclusive story. From their Special Correspondent, on May 6 1929, they published 'A TALE THAT JOSEPH CONRAD MIGHT HAVE WRITTEN'. Pemberton had talked. On another page in the paper, they actually had Pemberton's photograph. More convincing evidence had never been produced.

Pemberton, it was said, was then ninety-two years of age, still wearing the tailcoat in which he returned to

Liverpool fifty-seven years before, direct from the drama of *Mary Celeste*. He celebrated the occasion by 'having his photey took, probably for the only time in his life'. He explained that he was the cook of *Mary Celeste*.

'As a boy in Liverpool, where my father was a well-known character known as the crossing sweeper of Bold Street, I knew often enough what it was to go hungry, and determined to be a cook, to be always near where the food is. And all my life, I've been a cook. Not, mind you, like some of these people who call themselves cooks today, but a real cook. True, the mate of the *Mary Celeste* – I called him 'Starlight' Hullock because of his red nose – used to refer to me as 'Young Poison', but that is a common enough reference at sea to a cook who is supposed to kill the crew, but it was a different thing altogether when I saw in an American magazine a few years ago that the real clue to the mystery of the *Mary Celeste* was that the cook, meaning me, poisoned everybody on board, threw the bodies overboard, and then fell in after them. That's why I am telling the true story now.'

John Pemberton evokes himself as a sweaty little man with a heavy moustache, dressed in slops, busying over a cast iron stove. 'Not many would have stomached what we had to eat. Salt junk mostly. Big chunks of half-crumbling fat. In the dark, it was luminous. Come to that, there wasn't many who would even step aboard the *Mary Celeste*. Her owners had been trying to knock the bottom out of her for years. I signed on because, at eighteen, as I was then, I didn't know nothing better. To start with, I was the only crew the captain had, except the first mate. His proper name was Toby Jackson Hullock, better known on the waterfront in New York as the Bully of Baltimore. I called him 'Starlight' because people who crossed him saw stars. He called me 'Young Poison,' I've told you that already, because he said that the food out of my galley was enough to poison anybody. He wasn't far wrong at that.

'If you'd asked me, when we were rotting on the quayside in New York in that winter of 1872 – that winter when the 'osses which pulled the buses all got a disease called the epizootic staggers – I'd have said that the *Mary Celeste* was fit only for the knacker's herself. But the cap'n – Captain Benjamin Briggs his name was – got boozing with a British master whose old tub was tied up nearby. Name of Morehouse. Master of a 'moucher' ship which had been lying empty in the harbour, except for the rats, for months.'

It is evening. Captain Briggs and Captain Morehouse roll arm-in-arm along the New York waterfront. They come aboard the Mary Celeste *and stumble down the companionway into the cabin. In the cabin, Captain Briggs, half-seas over, plants a bottle of whisky on the table. He spills drinks for the two of them*

BRIGGS: Then I'm agreed.

MOREHOUSE: Wha's agreed?

BRIGGS: You've got a drink haven't you?

MOREHOUSE: Agreed.

BRIGGS: Well?

MOREHOUSE: What were we talking about?

BRIGGS (*sinking a dram*): Let's get everything straightened out.

MOREHOUSE: Bristol fashion.

BRIGGS (*raising a finger*): Your ship, the *Dei Gratia*, has a crew; but no cargo. Right?

MOREHOUSE: Right, sir.

BRIGGS: My ship has a cargo: but no crew.

MOREHOUSE: Right again.

BRIGGS: Right, sir. The propos ... here, have another drink.

He offers Captain Morehouse the bottle by the neck.
Captain Morehouse helps himself liberally. Captain
Briggs, absent-mindedly, overfills his own glass.

BRIGGS: The Limey and the Yank. Two friends in need.
The propos..never mind that. The sishuasion is that
you lend me three men to help work my brig to the
Azores. In return you carry the cargo I can't manage
waiting on the quayside.

MOREHOUSE: Agreed.

BRIGGS: Then what are we arguing about? Hullock, my
mate, says that he can find three more seamen from
the boarding house keepers.

MOREHOUSE: You'd be better if you sailed without
Hullock.

BRIGGS (*on his dignity*): I'll thank you, Captain Morehouse, to mind your business. I'm the master of the
Mary Celeste.

MOREHOUSE (*climbing unsteadily to his feet*): You'd be
better without Hullock. All right, I's agreed. I'll rendez-
vous with you, when you arrive at Santa Maria. My
men will bring aboard their boxes tomorrow. I'll warn
them to look out for trouble.

BRIGGS (*muzzily*): There'll be no trouble. I've made up
my mind. With a light cargo, I can take my wife.

MOREHOUSE: No trouble?

Captain Morehouse rolls out of the cabin. Captain
Briggs pours another drink. He is leaning drunkenly
over the table as there is a thump on the upper deck.
Gathering himself, he follows Captain Morehouse
up the companionway. The paraffin lamps in the
cabin throw a soft light on to the deck. In the gleam
of it, Hullock the mate fells a man with his fist and,
seizing his legs, hauls him forrard.

BRIGGS: What are you doing, Hullock?

HULLOCK: We've got the beginnings of a crew. And we've
got another one who's come willingly.

A third man appears out of the darkness with an exploded lip and a bashed face. He is a villainous character, dragging a seaman's chest who, with a push, tumbles the drunken captain on to his back. Heedless, he makes his way forward to the fo'c'sle. Captain Briggs, a frightened image of a man, crawls to his feet again. Hullock, his first mate, is a formidable figure, 'a six feet lump of mahogany'. He is in his forties, wearing a short-fitting monkey jacket which emphasises his bulging muscles. The immediate impression is of some awful all-in wrestler. The mate hooks on his cap, rolls a quid of tobacco round his mouth, and spits expertly on the cabin deck. Hullock keel-hauls an insensitive giant, with a mane of yellow hair, into the fo'c'sle. The job done, he pushes back his cap, and wipes the sweat off his brow. Then he spits contemptuously on the prostrate figure. Pemberton, the cook, makes his own comment.

PEMBERTON: It was Hullock, the mate, as hard as only an American mate can be – not Cap'n Briggs – who had the *Mary Celeste* under his thumb. It was obvious there'd be trouble when he shanghaied one man, and brought in another, two others in the end, you wouldn't trust with a carving knife. Hullock believed that he could tame them.

As Hullock stands over the prostrate man (his name is Carl Venholdt) in the foc's'le, the third ruffian arrives dragging his chest, and smiles evilly over his shoulder.

HULLOCK: I can do that to you, too.

He spits again. By way of echo, Pemberton in his galley spits in a sizzling saucepan. By contrast with Hullock, he is a tiny man with a miserable drooping adolescent moustache. He busies himself with cook's business as he talks. Captain Briggs stands on the maindeck, with Hullock beside him, watching the piano come aboard.

PEMBERTON: I've always hated tall men. Troublemakers, every one I ever met. Muscle-bound bullies like Hullock. I've outlived them all. Yet you know what caused the real trouble on the *Mary Celeste*? It wasn't them at all. It was this. . . .

The cottage piano swings on a hoist over the Mary Celeste's *decks. It sways about clumsily as men on the ropes strain to control it.*

PEMBERTON: A music box, a pianny – the sort that they used to call in the Yankee free-and-easies 'A Parlour Poll'. There's the toy which explains the mystery of the *Mary Celeste*. You'll be told that Mrs Briggs had a baby aboard. She hadn't. This was 'The Baby'.

HULLOCK (*aggressively*): What do you want 'the music' for?

BRIGGS: My wife won't travel without her piano.

HULLOCK: You still want her to sail with us?

BRIGGS (*contentedly looking up at the piano swinging over the deck*): Of course. I'm expecting her any minute now.

HULLOCK: With these murdering crimpers aboard?

BRIGGS: I shall expect you to deal with that.

HULLOCK: You know the sort of thing that happens on hen frigates?

BRIGGS: See to the piano. I think my wife is arriving.

A little woman – someone that Dickens might have invented – with a parasol on her arm and a big hat, trips to the ship's side, with a porter behind her wheeling a valise on a trolley. Captain Briggs goes to welcome her as the piano is lowered humpily on to the deck. Hullock contemptuously watches it settle. Then, turning his quid of tobacco, he looks omin-

*ously over his shoulder at Captain and Mrs Briggs.
His eyes range on to the rigging. A hand on the
yardarm is unfurling the sails.*

  *Mary Celeste sails along in a stiff breeze. From the
cabin below comes the sound of hymn music. Mrs
Briggs, playing the piano, is singing in a raucous
voice. Captain Briggs is on the poop. Hullock, sitting
on the step of it, is spitting moodily. Briggs, he has
only a pace or two to walk, joins him.*

BRIGGS (*cheerfully*): Well, we're on our way. I don't like
the weather outlook. But we've got a crew, and a full
cargo.

HULLOCK: And a foul-smelling cargo it is. And a stinking
crew. Three from that Limey ship. Three murdering
bastards from the boarding houses. You, me, Young
Poison the cook, and that hen of yours singing below
decks. Why doesn't she stop?

BRIGGS: Because....

HULLOCK: Because, my fanny. You know that I can't stow
my own sea chest because of that piano? Mark my
words, that hen of a wife of yours is going to make
trouble, the way aboard ships women always do. They'll
all want her.

BRIGGS: I'm the captain of this ship, Hullock.

HULLOCK (*unmoved*) You all say that. One of them'll
have her all the same. If you don't look out, they'll have
you in their way, too.

BRIGGS: I can look after myself.

HULLOCK (*rising to his feet*) Then look out now.

  *The formidable figure of Carl Venholdt, the man
who was shanghaied the night before, rolls out of the
fo'c'sle, and bears aft. Mrs Briggs is still bashing the
piano in the cabin. Hullock advances towards him.*

VENHOLDT: What am I doing here? I want to go back to
dry land.

HULLOCK: Forget that, we're going to make a seaman of you.

VENHOLDT: Who are you?

HULLOCK: You'll learn, squarehead.

VENHOLDT: So will you.

Threateningly, Venholdt strips off his shirt. Hullock slips off his monkey jacket. The two men measure up to each other like two hairy bears. Venholdt is the first to charge in. It is a bloody but unscientific fight. The music below decks stops. Mrs Briggs – a termagant in this version – appears up the companionway to throw everything in sight at the combatants. Captain Briggs has already joined in. After a break in the fight, Hullock settles the matter by grabbing a bucket, and crushing it over Venholdt's head. He drags him, half-conscious, to the forepeak to cool off in the wash of the sea.

The weather grows wilder. Pemberton, the cook, tries to control pots and pans throwing about the galley. The ruffian at the wheel is twisting the spokes uncertainly, watching the sea rather than the sails. Mrs Briggs, seemingly unaffected by the weather, is bashing out hymns on her piano in the cabin. Suddenly, the ship gives a sickening lurch – almost as if she is going on her beam ends. The piano breaks loose from its lashings, and Mrs Briggs is crushed underneath it in its fall.

Captain Briggs makes a headlong descent below. Unhurriedly, Hullock stations himself at the top of the companionway, looking down. Pemberton struggles with the mess in the galley. Others in the ship's company, sullenly and silently, straggle out to find out what's happened. Venholdt stirs on the forepeak like a stranded starfish, and crawls heavily to his knees. Pemberton peers out of the galley with a frying pan hanging in his hand.

Hullock, scarred with the marks of his fight with Venholdt, waits coolly at the top of the companionway for Captain Briggs. He glances challengingly over his shoulder at the half-circle of men gathering inquisitively about the mainmast behind him. Their hangdog air indicates that none of them is in a mood, after what has happened to Venholdt, to cross him. Captain Briggs, over the noise of the hostile sea, is heard slamming about in the cabin. He is presumably lifting the piano off the body of his wife. He comes on deck again, a man bereft of his senses.

BRIGGS: She's dead. My wife …
He looks about him until his eyes light on the man at the wheel.
BRIGGS: You did it! You killed my wife. (*to Hullock*) As the captain of the ship, I order you to throw that man overboard.

Hullock doesn't move. He simply watches the captain, attentively.

BRIGGS: So you won't do it. Then I will.

Captain Briggs makes across the poop, and engages the man at the wheel. Immediately, Hullock is after him. Seizing his shoulder, he throws Captain Briggs against the top gallant rail. Captain Briggs recovers himself. There is a brief roughhousing encounter between him and his first mate. Then Hullock manhandles him down the companionway into the cabin again. Disposed of the captain, he returns to the men looking on.

HULLOCK: Don't stand there staring. Back to your work! Or I'll thrash the hides off you. The lot of you. The lot of you – and I can.

They obviously believe him. The mate watches dourly as the crew breaks up and goes forrard. Then,

with a kick, he closes the door into the cabin.
The wind blows. Mary Celeste, racked with the strain,
rolls on in the heavy seas. It is night. Hullock is at the
wheel with a bottle in his free hand. At intervals he
takes a swig from the neck of it. In the little cabin
below the binnacle, it is plain that Captain Briggs is
on the bottle, too. There is the noise of heavy falls,
glass breaking, and muffled swearing. Noisily up the
companionway, Captain Briggs reels on to the deck.
He staggers towards Hullock.

BRIGGS: Dead, my darling wife. And you wouldn't kill
the man who did it.

HULLOCK: It wasn't the man at the wheel. It was the piano.
I told you not to bring it aboard.

He watches the set of the sails.

HULLOCK (*calmly*): You'd better ditch the piano.

BRIGGS (*wildly*): Throw it overboard?

HULLOCK: We can do it at the same time that we drop
your wife.

BRIGGS: You're not going to do that. My wife – in the
sea.

HULLOCK: We are, you know.

He pours down another dram from the neck of the
bottle. When Captain Briggs tries to interfere he
throws the drunken man out of his way with a push
of his arm. Captain Briggs collapses on the deck.
Hullock, working the wheel, spits on his captain.
Mary Celeste drives out of dark into light. Im-
probably, the ruffianly crew is, more or less
reverently, carrying a burden wrapped in canvas on
to the deck, and dropping it into the sea. Hullock
is controlling his captain by holding him round the
scruff of the neck. When the body has been com-
mitted to the sea, the crew carry the piano out of
the cabin, and pitch it after Mrs Briggs. The piano

bobs, unwilling to sink, in the wake of the ship. Captain Briggs struggles in hysterical tears. With horrible calm, Hullock sets him up, and knocks him down. Briggs falls on the deck.

HULLOCK (*to the crew*): You all know, if you don't know already, who's boss here now.

SEAMAN: It's mutiny!

HULLOCK (*looking at Briggs*): He's mad. (*to crew*) What we all want is a dram out of the cabin.

Hullock goes below. He hands bottles to welcoming hands. Then he knocks off the neck of another for himself. With the bottle in his hand, he comes on deck, and kicks the recumbent captain with his foot. Forrard, there is the noise of singing. The man at the wheel has a bottle, too. Hullock signals him forrard, and takes over the wheel himself. Mary Celeste sails on with the noise of a drunken crew in the fo'c'sle. The cook, Pemberton, is flat on his back in the galley with an empty bottle at the side of his bunk. Hullock, the man who looks his name, stands over the wheel. Mary Celeste sails on into the dark. Hullock, a shadow in the dawn, reels down towards the galley. He shakes Pemberton in his bunk.

HULLOCK: Wake up, you drunken swine. Where's Briggs? Where's the captain?

PEMBERTON (*disinterestedly, clinging to the warmth of the bunk*): How do I know? You saw him last.

HULLOCK: He isn't aboard.

PEMBERTON (*sitting up and rubbing his eyes*): The captain isn't aboard?

HULLOCK: No, he's gone. I've searched the ship for him. I thought he might be here.

PEMBERTON (*suspiciously*): You were at the wheel.

HULLOCK (*threateningly*): Are you suggesting I pushed him overboard?

PEMBERTON: I'm suggesting nothing. I'm only the cook, that's all I am, in this ship. But if Cap'n Briggs and his wife have both gone, it's trouble.

HULLOCK (*thoughtfully*): Yes – that's what people are going to say. Out of your bunk, Young Poison, and all hands aft. This is something we've all got to work out together.

As Hullock leaves the galley, he hammers with his huge fist on the shell of the deckhousing.

HULLOCK: All hands aft! All aft!

He reels through the waist of the ship and down the companionway into the cabin. The cabin now shows all the disorder of a debauch. Broken glasses and bottles roll about the deck. From an open locker, Hullock collects three more full bottles, and appears beside the mainmast as the evil-looking crew shuffle out of the fo'c'sle. Including Pemberton, excluding the man at the wheel, there are five of them. As they come towards him, Hullock throws the bottles to them to catch.

HULLOCK: Briggs doesn't need 'em. He's gone overboard.

He looks them over.

HULLOCK: Where's the squarehead?

SEAMAN (*grinning*): He says, if you want him, you can go and get him.

Aggressively, Hullock shoulders through the group on the tiny space of deck under the sails. Outside the entrance to the fo'c'sle, he encounters Carl Venholdt, with a bloody bandage wrapped about his head, and a wild gleam in his eye.

VENHOLDT: So you'll make a seaman of me!

He lets loose a wild punch which sends Hullock

*reeling on the deck against the ship's rail. Hullock
grimly gathers himself to his feet.*

HULLOCK: So you haven't had enough?

*As Hullock and Venholdt wrestle together, others
of the crew join in, with the apparent intention of
separating the combatants. One of them smacks a
bottle over Venholdt's scalp. Pemberton uses his
frying pan. The encounter ends with Venholdt splash-
ing overboard. Hullock, his face bloody, concludes
the matter by picking up his cap. None of them is
interested in the fate of Carl Venholdt.*
*A seaman, wiping blood off his face, addresses
Hullock.*

SEAMAN: Did you push Briggs overboard, too?

HULLOCK: He was drunk and he was mad. He chucked
himself into the sea after his hen.

SEAMAN (*cynically*): Who's going to believe that?

HULLOCK: Who's going to believe anything that's happened on this cursed brig?

He stares at the rest of them, accusingly.

HULLOCK: They'll call us all murderers.

*The men shift their feet anxiously. Hullock, his
authority established, becomes confidential.*

HULLOCK: Face facts. We know the truth of it; but who
else does? Who else will believe us? Me, I'm for leaving
this ship soon as we sight dry land. The rest of you, if
you value your skins, will follow me. Think it over.

*Turning his back on them, he goes below. The
tatterdemalion crew, what's left of them, stare at
each other in surprise.*
*The ship, white sails bellying, is in sunnier seas. Gulls
are wheeling and mewing overhead. A bight of land,
one of the islands of the Azores, lies to the port of*

her. Three men – one of them Hullock – are unlash-
ing the ship's boat of the Mary Celeste, *on the main*
hatch. A fourth seaman looks on with his hands
planted firmly in his pockets.

HULLOCK (*to the seaman looking on*): Changed your mind?

SEAMAN: No, we're going back where we comes from.
To the ship we ought never have left. The *Dei Gratia.*

HULLOCK: After the weather we've had, she's probably
followed Captain Briggs to the bottom.

SEAMAN: We'll take a chance on that.

The seaman leaves them to put his head in the galley,
where Pemberton is peeling potatoes.

SEAMAN: They're launching the boat. You going, Young
Poison?

PEMBERTON: I'm staying here. They'll come back.

SEAMAN: We're not waiting. You'll have to help with the
sailing of the ship.

PEMBERTON: You sound as if you want to get rid of me.

SEAMAN: All the rest have gone. You're not one of the
Dei Gratia crew.

PEMBERTON: I'm staying. So that's that.

The other two men, with Hullock, have dropped into
the ship's boat and are pulling away from the shore.
The three remaining seamen, with Pemberton, watch
her go. There one of them runs up the ratlines to un-
furl sail. Another goes to the wheel. Mary Celeste,
after the heave to, is on her way again. The chief
seaman is in the cabin calculating his position on the
chart. Seemingly satisfied, he goes on deck and hangs
over the rail.
Captain Morehouse is standing at the rail of the Dei
Gratia, *looking through his glass at the horizon. The*
mate Deveau is behind him.

MOREHOUSE: That's the *Celeste*, Deveau.

DEVEAU (*borrowing the glass*): I believe you're right.

MOREHOUSE: She didn't make Santa Maria (*taking the glass back again*) but it's her all right. Heave to, and make towards her.

DEVEAU: Aye, aye.

Captain Morehouse keeps his eyes out to sea. On the deck of the Mary Celeste, *the seaman is pointing out to Pemberton the other ship on the skyline.*

SEAMAN (*on the* Mary Celeste): It's her all right. It's the *Dei Gratia.* I'd know her anywhere. We've found her.

He turns to the man at the wheel.

SEAMAN: Hard over.

MOREHOUSE (*through speaking trumpet*): Brig ahoy! Ahoy!

A voice answers distantly over the Atlantic wastes. 'Ahoy!'

MOREHOUSE (*to Deveau*): Make the yawl ready. I'm going to board her.

A ship's boat is seen pulling across the open sea, two men rowing and Captain Morehouse sitting in the stern. Captain Morehouse clambers aboard the Mary Celeste, *and goes into the cabin. The ship rolls indeterminately in the swell. Morehouse sits in the cabin with the three seamen, and Pemberton.*

MOREHOUSE: So that's it. The only crew left on the *Mary Celeste* is the crew of the *Dei Gratia.*

SEAMAN: Except Pemberton.

MOREHOUSE: I'll come to him. We can legally run the *Mary Celeste* into Gibraltar as a derelict. In my judgement, we're entitled to salvage.

SEAMAN: What about Pemberton?

MOREHOUSE (*looking at Pemberton*): For you it's a matter of keeping your mouth shut; or facing a charge of murder. I'll make a deal with you. I'll take you aboard the *Dei Gratia* to Gibraltar; and I'll pay your passage back home to wherever you come from.... where do you come from?

PEMBERTON (*miserably*): Liverpool.

MOREHOUSE: You know that, if you talk, nobody will believe you.

PEMBERTON: I know. That's what the mate said.

MOREHOUSE: All right. Wind's getting up again. Let's get under way.

Captain Morehouse gets purposefully to his feet.

MOREHOUSE: You get in the ship's boat with me, Pemberton.

If Laurence Keating had published his story anonymously, and without comment, it might now enjoy the same sort of prestige as Conan Doyle's. I have written only the bare bones of it; but it is composed with even more colourful exuberance than 'J. Habakuk Jephson's Statement'. In some respects, it is the more convincing. But Keating wasn't content with the role of a storyteller. He had to underline that what he had written was 'a famous sea mystery exposed'. He exposed himself in the blurb of his publisher (Heath Cronton):

'*Unnumbered guesses have been made, unnumbered writers have attempted imaginary solutions of the problem. But what, after all, really did happen?*

'*The book, The Great Mary Celeste Hoax, tells us. The account, compiled for the first time from official sources, relates an astonishing case of successful hoodwinking. The mystery goes; instead, there emerges an epic story of the sea which would have delighted Clark Russell. Years of labour, involving research at Gibraltar, New York, Genoa, and a host of places on the Atlantic seaboard, have gone to the making of the following pages and have resulted in this – the greatest detective story of the sea. It is more than that, more than a thrilling detective story in real life, it is a human drama of singular interest.*

What happened to the crew of the Mary Celeste? The answer is given in the following pages by one of the survivors – for a survivor there was. In some respects it is a disturbing recital. In others, it depicts those unfortunate people as puppets of a malignant Fate.

'Those who like a grim, true story of the sea will enjoy the book; those – and there are many – who are steeped in the history of the Mary Celeste – will be startled by the true explanation of those baffling features which have made the strange affair the Sea's most insoluble puzzle.

'An absorbing book!'

*'*REX CLEMENTS *(Author of a "A Gipsy of the Horn" etc.), who read the book in* MS *form and advised the publishers thereon, writes: I have, I think, read nearly everything of importance hitherto published with reference to the story of the Mary Celeste. In my opinion Mr Keating has here given the final explanation of the mystery, and I cordially recommend the book on the subject.'*

To many people at the time, I include myself, it seemed that Pemberton's story could be the last word. It explained so much: how a ship could sail for hundreds of miles apparently without anybody aboard her. It confirmed the theory, current at the time, of mutiny and a salvage conspiracy. It offered a reason why the surviving members of the crew had kept silence so long.

I was then editing the *Strand Magazine* which had done so much to immortalise the great story. I was sufficiently curious to put a small advertisement, asking what had happened to Laurence J. Keating, in the personal column of *The Times*. In reply, I had a letter from a sister of his in Liverpool telling me that he had died, 'he was a decent fellow', a few years earlier. I also had a letter from a bibliophile friend in Edinburgh, Councillor Patrick Murray, enclosing a pamphlet on the case written by a New Englander named Charles Edey Fay. Fay told a very different story.

It is an element in the work of a writer that years can pass between the conception of a notion, and a conclusion. Often, there is no conclusion. I think that it was J. M. Barrie who said that he had ten plays in his head for every one he had written. All authors fail to complete all that they contemplate. I nearly forgot *Mary Celeste*. But, like a mistress of the past, her memory remained warm in my mind.

In 1957, I was seduced by her again. I find that I wrote a letter to the editor of the *Liverpool Daily Post*:

'Sir – I am making some research for a projected book into the fascinating mystery of the Mary Celeste, the brigantine which was found in 1872, sailing the seas in good order without a soul aboard her. In the controversy which has raged over the case ever since, one of the most discussed solutions was written by Laurence J. Keating, who published a book in 1929 called 'The Great Mary Celeste Hoax'.

'Keating's theory was that when the brigantine was found, supposedly derelict by the British ship Dei Gratia, she was in fact manned by four men who went across to the Dei Gratia to enable the British captain to bring her into port and claim salvage money.

'Keating's claim was that two of the men who were aboard her were Liverpool men; the ship's cook, a man named John Pemberton, and the ship's bos'n whose name was Jack Dossell. According to Keating, Pemberton, then over eighty, was alive "near Liverpool" in 1929. He was born in Bolton Street, I gather, in 1847.

'Jack Dossell, according to Keating, finished up pedalling ointments and quack medicines along the Liverpool Docks and then further afield. He was also known as a fiery street corner theologian under the soubriquet of Hellfire Jack.

'So far, my attempts to trace somebody who might have a recollection of these men have failed. More than that, I

haven't yet been able to trace anybody who remembers Laurence Keating himself. He lived in Liverpool, and may well have died in the city.

'If any of your readers can give me any information about any one of these three Liverpool men, they may well contribute something to the unpicking of a bird's nest of mystery which has been collecting ever since that ship of mystery, the "Mary Celeste", was brought into Gibraltar Harbour at Christmastime, eighty-five years ago.'

I had one reply; but it was a significant one. It came from Captain T. E. Elwell in the Isle of Man. He had met Keating, he said, who shared the interest of a friend of his, Frederick Flaherty, in the mystery. Flaherty's guess was that the answer was a conspiracy to get salvage money. Keating seized on the notion as a theme of a book. He was 'the worst type of Liverpool Irishman' said Captain Elwell. And, in due course, Captain Elwell sent me a copy of *The Great Mary Celeste Hoax*, inscribed by Laurence J. Keating to his friend and colleague, Frederick Flaherty, which Flaherty had later sent, with a letter of disgust, to Captain Elwell. I have it now, its text littered on the edges, in shaky handwriting, with corrections and expletives.

Myself, I am reluctant to condemn Keating out of hand. He was a penurious journalist who thought he was clever enough to fool the world. In fairness he nearly pulled it off. He wrote an exciting story, which was accepted as truth by people who ought to have known better. There are still those who believe it. His mistake was that he did it almost too well; and he backed out too late.

When a reporter from the *Evening Standard* arrived in Liverpool in the hope of interviewing the cook, John Pemberton, Keating somehow fobbed him off. When Captain Elwell sought to interview the survivor, reputedly an inmate of Belmont Road (now Newsham Hospital) Pemberton had conveniently died. It is correct that Keating's 'friend and colleague', Frederick Flaherty, was present when the *Standard*'s representative appeared. It is certain that that newspaperman never wrote the story.

The story, which appeared in the paper from 'our special correspondent' was written by Laurence Keating himself. The picture purporting to be of John Pemberton when he arrived home at Liverpool was, in fact, a studio photograph of Keating's own father.

10. THE SHIP'S COMPANY

The essence of the imposters' claims was that the crew of the *Mary Celeste* was not the ship's company she was supposed to have had. The view was expressed in the letter to the literary journal, *John O'London's Weekly*, in 1927 (*see page* 17). It was suggested that no one knew, in 1872, who was aboard a ship for certain until she sailed; and perhaps never after. There could be an element of fact in it. After all, the press gang was not so far out of date. But I have a strong suspicion that 'William Adams', who wrote to *John O'London's*, had a vested interest in exploiting the query. My guess is that he was Laurence J. Keating, writing under another pseudonym.

No reasonable person can doubt who was aboard the *Mary Celeste*. The official list of the persons composing the crew was issued in New York in November, 1872. Benjamin S. Briggs, her master, had enlisted Albert G. Richardson of Stockton Springs, Maine, as first mate. According to the crew list of November 4, 1872, made by Mr H. E. Jenks, Deputy United States Shipping Commissioner, Richardson was 28 years of age, 5 feet 8 inches tall, with light complexion and brown hair; wages $50 a month. The second mate was Andrew Gilling, birthplace New York; aged 25; height 5 feet 8 inches; complexion, light; hair, light; wages $35. The steward and cook, Edward William Head, was born in New York, age 23, height 5 feet 8 inches; complexion, light; hair, light; wages per month $40.

The remaining members of the crew were German seamen. It is possible that the American official who recorded them got the spelling of some of their names wrong. But they appear to have been Volkert Lorenzen (29), Adrian Martens (35), Bob Lorenzen (25) and Gottlieb Goodschaad

(23). The Germans came from the small islands of Föhr and Amru in East Prussia. There is every reason to suppose that they were decent fellows. Before they left the East River Pier Mrs Briggs wrote to her mother-in-law: 'Benjamin thinks that we have got a pretty peaceable set this time all around, if they continue as they have begun. Can't tell yet how smart they are.'

I quote Charles Edey Fay, to whom I shall refer again later: 'There can be no question about the *Mary Celeste* being adequately manned. She carried a crew of eight, including the captain, which was in conformity with the recommendations of a Seamen's Congress held some years later in England, when a total of seven was recommended for sailing vessels of 200 tons register, and a crew of nine, all told, for vessels of 300 tons. It is reasonable to assume that Captain Briggs, experienced mariner that he was, would exercise more than ordinary care in the selection of the crew for a voyage on which his wife and two-year-old daughter were to accompany him.' He left his son Arthur, who was aged seven, to start his schooling. When Captain Briggs took command of the *Mary Celeste*, he was in his thirty-eighth year.

It is proper to tell that, in the subsequent enquiry, there was evidence of doubt in the court that the ship's company were all whom they were said to be. Mr Solly Flood may have been over-enthusiastic. When Captain Winchester was called as witness he was confronted with photographs.

'*The photograph now shown me is of Captain Oliver Briggs, Benjamin Briggs' brother. So is the second photograph. This one is that of Captain Benjamin Briggs, the master of the Mary Celeste. I do not know the maiden name of Mrs Briggs, wife of Benjamin Briggs, but he told me that she was a minister's daughter. I do not see a photograph of her in this book.*

'*I also knew the mate Richardson. He was the husband of my wife's niece, a man of excellent character. He was*

*an experienced and courageous officer in whom I had
great confidence. I believe that he had presence of mind.
His three previous captains spoke of him as fit to command
any ship, and I believe that he would not leave his ship
except for life or death.'*

The Imperial German Consul, at *Utersum auf Föhr*
took a hand in the matter. He was properly concerned with
the fate of the three German, or Danish, seamen. On
February 7, 1885, he wrote to the American Consul, Mr
Horatio Sprague:

'Highly esteemed Mr Consul,

*... Before all I must give you some information respect-
ing our local circumstances stating that the island of Föhr
is scarcely 172 miles large and has not even 5000 inhabitants from which only 130 souls fall to the lot of the
village Utersum. The foregoing will prove you that all
inhabitants of our village are not only known to me by
their names but also are personally acquainted with me.
The neighbouring Island of Amrum scarcely shows the
number of 600 inhabitants from which the greater part of
the male population are likewise personally known to me.
In consequence whereof it is not strange nor at all surprising if the personalities of the three missed people can
be described by me, the more so as I have stated formerly
that the two from this place were my former school
comrades.*

Ferdinand Schott.
'Imperial German Consul'

T. A. Nickelsen, Chief of the Parish of *Utersum*, Isle
of Föhr, Prussia, wrote, too. His letter is dated 1873.

*'... Neither to this place nor to Amrum ever any notice
has reached respecting the fate of the three seamen missing, the relatives know as little about the missing men as
myself. The mother of the two brethren (Volkert and
Bob Lorenzen) is still living and she does not cease to
deplore the loss of her two sons. The eldest of whom was*

married, his wife and daughter are still living here in poor circumstances. The younger brother was betrothed and his bride has married another seaman and also lives in this village.... Of the effects of the two brethren Lorenzen nothing has reached home just because one supposes that it was not worthwhile claiming them. A short time before they got on board the Mary Celeste both brethren had lost all their clothing and sundry other effects through shipwreck and some could therefore be provided with only the most necessary articles.... The foregoing is more or less all I know respecting the men, but I must add hereto that same had enjoyed for their class as seamen an extraordinarily good education, which is generally the case in all our islands. That some must have lost their lives, I take as a fact, but I cannot admit that they have had a share in any act of violence or in any mutiny which is guaranteed to me the character of the men in question who were of a most pacific disposition.

> *Yours most devoted friend,*
> *T. A. Nickelsen.*
> *Chief of the Parish'*

With its slightly faulty English, the letter from the Parish Clerk shows clearly that the German seamen were reliable local fellows, good islanders with a foot in the land who could be trusted. There seems no doubt that the crew were exactly whom they were said to be. But, years later, Mr Solly Flood was still pursuing his curiously vindictive prosecution. I suspect that, like so many have before and since, he suffered from a fixation in which his first thoughts became his last ones. He certainly seems to have made an intolerable nuisance of himself. He had got it into his Irish head that, when *Mary Celeste* came under his legal authority, he was uncovering a conspiracy. None can say now that he was right. It was just a bit of a bore that, like a toothless terrier with an old rat, he wouldn't let go.

Thirteen years after the enquiry was over, he was still at it. He wrote a letter to Consul Sprague in January 9, 1885, and a postscript on February 20, in which he made a surprising demand for legal costs from the U.S. Government for his efforts on behalf of Captain Briggs.* He also protested that the private property of the crew, which had been released by the court, had been returned to their relations. The melodeon, and the notorious sword, had been shipped, with Captain and Mrs Briggs private effects, to his brother in New Bedford, Massachusetts. In Mr Solly Flood's opinion, all should have remained within the custody of the court. The American consul's job, in his judgement, was simply to find houseroom for them.

By that time Mr Solly Flood had retired from his post. Mr Sprague reporting to the Assistant Secretary of State in Washington, permitted himself at the end of his official communication (No. 488 on the subject), dated 4 March, 1885, a pawky comment:

'In conclusion, I would beg to state confidentially that Mr Flood is an Irish gentleman. Although reported as being over eighty years of age, he has always been considered as an individual of very vivid imagination, and to have survived, to some extent at least, the judicious application of his mental faculties. Such is, I believe, the general opinion of the community at large, even among his most intimate and personal friends.'

I would have liked to have written that. I wish I had known that dry American, Mr Horatio J. Sprague, the consul. In a small world he was one who had his feet firmly on the ground.

---

* In the appendices, I have reproduced the long letter in full. It is not without relevance to the case, or the people connected with it.

11 . THE LIARS AND THE
THEORISTS

The imposters are easily dismissed. 'Abel Fosdyk,' judged solely by his lack of maritime knowledge, never mind his ignorance of the timber and sail of the ship in which he reputedly served, was clearly a show-off who knew nothing of the ways of the sea. 'Triggs' story, involving the discovery of a derelict steamer loaded with gold, and so rusted that they could not read her name, is plainly ridiculous. It suggests that Captain Briggs, with his wife and infant daughter, would voluntarily abandon his ship, in which he had a material interest worth much more than the £1,200 he is supposed to have had off the derelict, and exile himself and his family from New England where he had a home. Keating's account, which was so widely accepted, was no more than an impudent trick by a man, not without imaginative ability, who thought that he was cleverer than 'them'. He reveals himself in his personal letters in which he refers to a book as 'a buke'. It wasn't a bad word for what he wrote.

Yet, such is the wide-eyed credulity of editors, such the anxiety to find a good story, that in every case, in newspapers and periodicals, the imposters got a hearing. The defence, of course, is that if a man chooses to tell a big enough lie, the lie makes news in itself. But in the ephemeral world of journalism there is seldom, except under legal pressure, a retraction. There is no headline in the story 'which-was-not'. Thus, so many tales are never awarded an ending. Thus, so many readers believe what they have been conned into believing by the printed word.

On first thought it is singular that *Mary Celeste* stands

out as the first mystery of the sea. In fact vessels found
with no one aboard them have been as common as black-
birds. There have been many *Mary Celestes*. I recollect a
splendid short story by Oliver Onions in which, in a
transfer of time, a submarine commander of today encounters an Elizabethan galleon. When he hails the strange
old ship, from another century, the last survivor of her
crew, hoarse with thirst in a sunbaked sea, achieves in his
death rattle an answer. He calls that this ship sailed from
the same home port in England as the submarine. His
name is the submarine commander's own.

The story is not irrelevant. The mystery of *Mary
Celeste* is largely a mystery of wish. It seems that it is
endemic in us to look for a tall tale; that it is a human
need, like the dogmas of religion. An ocean puzzle, it has
been elevated by seamen, notorious inventors of tales, out
of all reality. I often wonder what lies the old sailor told
the Young Raleigh in Millais's picture.

During World War II I was attached for a time to the
Royal Navy. It was a rule that all letters home from the
crew had to be read, for security. I was asked to help. It
was extraordinary what exploits of sea battle and adventure, all born of their simple imaginations, the sailors
described to their folks at home; in the knowledge, too,
that wartime censorship required that their letters would
be read by their officers in the Ward Room. We passed
them all. We passed them because they could only have
foxed the enemy.

Mary Celeste undoubtedly achieved the magnetic interest she has, amongst all the stories of the sea, for the
reason that the long legislative procedure at Gibraltar
brought her to notice. She was lifted into immortality
by Arthur Conan Doyle. She has been used by every
subsequent romancer to float another bubble.

One of the most transparent made a brief appearance
in the *Nautical Magazine* of December, 1913. The author
was, this time, a Russian, Captain Lukhmanoff, who

claimed to have had the story from an old Greek sailor, Demetrius Specioti. Demetrius told him that he had been a saloon keeper in Boston and had shipped in the *Mary Celeste* under an assumed name. During the voyage the brigantine, which he described as a long sharp ship with rakish stem and masts, was unlucky enough to encounter a pirate. Her crew was impressed to replace fever casualties. But the fever spread. Captain Briggs, his wife and child, and nearly all her hands died. Finally, at the very moment when Demetrius and the men from the *Mary Celeste* had organised themselves, rather late in the day, to deal with their captors, the pirate ship was run down by an Italian steamer. Demetrius was the sole survivor.

J. G. Lockhart, dealing with the more extravagant of the faked solutions, tells that he was sent a photograph of a message in cipher which was sent to the office of the *Gibraltar Chronicle:* 'It was accompanied by a letter from one Ramon Alvarado, of Cincinnati, Ohio; dated August 10, 1909, which informed the newspaper that the key to the mystery of the *Mary Celeste* was to be found in the cipher message. This was apparently written in some sort of shorthand. So far, no one has been successful in decoding it.

There was another. Mr R. E. Greenhough revealed that, in 1904 or 1905, while serving as an apprentice in the Swansea barque *Ardorinha*, bound for Chile, he was one of a party put ashore to fetch sand from a group of tiny islands known as St Paul's. '*The party, on landing, came across a skeleton, propped against a rock, with a bottle nearly filled with discoloured paper, which when taken out was found to be covered with writing. As the writing was in a language which no one could understand, no further attention was paid to it. Mr Greenhough, however, kept the paper; and many years later found someone to decipher and translate it.*

'*The writing was in German, and Mr Greenhough gave*

some extracts: "I am dying. My ship struck these rocks at dawn three days ago. She sank immediately. Only 1 of all her crew reached the shore alive. There is no water. I am dying of thirst. It has been a voyage of disaster.'

Incoherently, befitting a dying man, he went on to tell that the steamer in which he had sailed had lost three men killed in the engine room. They had forgotten to wind the chronometer, the only one on the ship. They were too weak to get steam on the boilers.

"Knew must ask assistance to take us to Gibraltar for crew. That was ruin. Ship not insured . . . Early morning sighted small brig becalmed . . . The mate said "Take her crew.' "

Of course it was the *Celeste. "Went aboard. Captain asked why we came. His wife and child were with him. It was hard. It would have been easy without the woman. But the mate got behind the captain, he and two others, and threw him. His wife fainted. Then we pointed pistols. Crew went into boat quietly. One man shot. He fell into the sea. We left no one aboard."*

I have left out much of the detail. The story is interesting only for what people can be persuaded to believe. Messages in bottles, dying testaments under oath, skeletons on the rocks, pirates and fever, cipher messages and improbably desert-island treasure-island places are the stuff of fiction which, in uneventful lives, people are happy to pass as truth. It is a diversion that the only message in a bottle of which I can speak with authority ran: 'We are emigrants to Australia. The food aboard this ship is lousy.'

Yet fantasy always wins. I suppose that it is a happy thing that it should. Nothing, says J. G. Lockhart, was so fantastic as the explanation of the mystery of *Mary Celeste* which appeared in the *British Journal of Astrology*, and which gave the entire episode of *Mary Celeste* a mystical experience, connecting it, by processes of reasoning beyond the power of ordinary human understanding, with the Great Pyramid of Gizeh, the lost continent of Atlantis, and the British Israel movement.

In the hunt for an explanation of the ship's abandonment, it was suggested that she might have encountered an iceberg (almost impossible so far south); that the crew mutinied in drunkenness (no drink aboard apart from crude alcohol); that they were reduced by fever, or that the captain went mad. L. du Garde Peach, in a highly successful B.B.C. radio play in 1923 amusingly resurrected the theory that the crew were picked off, one by one, by the tentacles of a giant octopus. It was an explanation of the axe-mark, one of the crew hitting back on the ship's rail. Like Conan Doyle, du Garde Peach never pretended that he was writing other than fiction. But, like Conan Doyle, it was widely believed, in the big world of radio at that time, that he told truth. As late as 1946, one of the wilder solutions suggested was when people on both sides of the Atlantic were reporting the appearance of Flying Saucers. It was solemnly proposed that the crew of the *Mary Celeste* were lifted off into outer space.

Enough of the nonsense. Unquestionably, the most serious study of the case has been made by Mr Charles Edey Fay, whose superbly documented book, published in a limited edition by the Peabody Museum of Salem, Massachusetts in 1942, includes nearly everything that is known about *Mary Celeste*. My criticism of the author is that he is perhaps too anxious to present his fellow New Englanders in the bright light of the Pilgrim Fathers. Nobody, least of all a sea captain, could have been quite as holy as he paints Captain Briggs. Still, what follows is a healthy contrast to what has gone before. My own comments can wait. This is the picture of Briggs and his wife which their descendants and relations have presented to the world. . . .

AMERICAN VOICE: Born of sturdy, God-fearing New England stock; reared in an atmosphere of wholesome refinement, and trained as well in the salty curriculum of the sea as in ways of right living, Benjamin Briggs was well prepared to undertake the responsibilities of the command of *Mary Celeste*.

Briggs goes below and joins his wife and child in the cabin. His wife is working at her sewing machine. His daughter is on the floor playing with alphabet bricks. The captain embraces both of them. The mood is Dickens, or Samuel Smiles, at his worst.

AMERICAN VOICE: Benjamin and his wife Sarah, to whom he had been united in marriage, when she was twenty and he twenty-seven, were deeply devoted to each other. They had been boy and girl sweethearts. She was the daughter of a parson of the Congregational Church of Marion. Benjamin was familiar with the Bible, which he read regularly. No grog was allowed aboard his ship. His last thought, when he sailed, was to write a letter to his old mother.

The last man, you would have supposed, to be involved in the greatest mystery of the sea. So what happened to an upright and downright New Englander, an experienced seaman, a man of God with his wife and child sailing with him, to lead him to abandon his ship. A cousin of his, a cousin of his wife's too, made this suggestion:

Mrs Briggs, sitting at the melodeon in the captain's cabin, is selecting sheets of music. Captain Briggs is leaning over her attentively. The baby is playing on the floor.

MRS BRIGGS: Let's have the new one, 'Little Brown Jug'.
CAPTAIN BRIGGS: At this time of morning, my dear, I was thinking that it might be more appropriate if we sang a hymn. We don't want to bring up young Sophy with the wrong notions.

MRS BRIGGS: At her age, she doesn't know the difference.

CAPTAIN BRIGGS: Very well. I'm not sure I know all the words of this new fangled ditty. But there's nothing better on a long voyage than a good sing.

MRS BRIGGS (*settling over the melodeon*): I knew you'd agree, darling.

> *She plays the opening bars. Captain Briggs tucks his handkerchief into his sleeve, braces his shoulders, and presses the points of his fingers to the family Bible hard beside him. Mrs Briggs takes her hands momentarily off the keys.*

MRS BRIGGS: I'm glad the crew is a smart lot.

CAPTAIN BRIGGS: We haven't had real hard weather yet. We shall see.

MRS BRIGGS (*looking at the baby*): Sophy is loving it.

CAPTAIN BRIGGS (*putting his arm round her shoulder*): My life is to make you both happy, my dear.

> *Mrs Briggs happily presses the keys again. The two of them join enthusiastically in a rendering of 'Little Brown Jug'. They are in full sing when a muffled explosion trembles through the ship. Captain Briggs, the perfect master, has put his hat on before the mate, Albert Richardson, bursts into the cabin.*

RICHARDSON: Forehatch blown off, sir. Cargo looks like sending us all to the bottom.

> *Captain Briggs is quickly on deck, with Richardson close behind him. There's a rumbling inside the ship, and fumes of smoke grow out of the forward hatch. Seamen are anxiously checking the pumps.*

CAPTAIN BRIGGS: I ought never to have carried a cargo of crude alcohol. She'll blow up – and with my wife and baby aboard. Lower the boat.

RICHARDSON (*shouting*): Stand by to lower the boat.

*The hands rip off the top gallant rail on the port
side. They sling the boat off her seating on the mainmast hatch, and lower her overboard. Mrs Briggs
with the baby in her arms, comes on deck.*

CAPTAIN BRIGGS (*embracing her*): It'll all be all right,
dear. You just get into the boat with Sophy. We'll hang
on to our ship, until we're certain everything is safe,
with a line.

RICHARDSON: There's a coil of rope in the forehatch.

CAPTAIN BRIGGS: Never mind that. Lash us on to the peak
halliard. You can run it through the top gallant rail.

RICHARDSON (*busying himself on the job*): Aye, aye, sir.

*Captain Briggs, comfortingly, sees his wife and
daughter overboard into the open boat, bouncing beside the* Mary Celeste. *Then he rushes back to his
cabin for his chronometers. Meanwhile the whole
crew have gone over the side. Captain Briggs is the
last to leave. The yawl – 16 to 20 feet long with 9 to
12 inches freeboard carrying ten people – drifts away,
off to port, at the end of the long towline.*
*In a sudden squall in the grey weather, the rope,
holding the open boat to the ship, parts. The ship
reels on. The rowboat turns over in the troubled sea.
The people aboard her are lost.*

It is something of a pity that the most ordinary explanation of the fate of the crew seems to be the most likely
one. I cannot believe that Captain Benjamin Briggs, re-
joicing in his Puritan Christian name, was quite as holy
as the New Englanders represent him to have been. If he
was, a little sin would have done him good. With a bit of
the devil in him he would not have abandoned his ship.
Yet, if you dismiss the romancers, that is probably what
happened.

Charles Edey Fay records that, during the summer of

1930, Captain Henry O. Appleby told him that escaping gas in the cargo of alcohol may have caused an explosion, frightening all hands, and causing them to take to the boat. 'He said that while in command of the *Daisy Boynton*, on a voyage to Bilbao, Spain, with a cargo of petroleum, gases blew the hatches off and steam or vapour, accompanied by a crackling sound, began to come from the vessel's hold. The crew came running aft, and urged Captain Appleby to lower the boats, believing the ship to be on fire. The captain reassured them by explaining that the dunnage, consisting of pine wood, several cords of it from the south, loaded during cold weather with frost in it, would sometimes crackle that way and make a noise, like that of fire, when the vessel encountered warmer temperatures. He told them that they were in no greater danger than he was, and thereby succeeded in calming them.'

A letter to Edey Fay from Mrs Thomas J. Port, daughter of Captain Appleby, stated: '*My father's theory was that the dunnage wood was covered with ice when it was put aboard, and that as the ice melted it made vapour with the fumes of the alcohol with which she was loaded, and then blew off the forehatch which was found on the deck beside the opening. The people, fearing a general explosion, took to one of the boats. He said that Captain Winchester told him he had put aboard a new boat which was missing when the brig was brought in. The fore-brace was trailing over the side when they found her, and my father believed they were fast to it, intending to go back aboard if nothing more happened, when a sudden squall struck the brig and they had to let go to avoid being towed under. They lost the ship – couldn't keep near her; and eventually perished.*'

In *Yachting*, February, 1940, Dr Oliver W. Cobb of Easthampton, Massachusetts who was a cousin of Captain Briggs and also of the captain's wife, who was Sarah Elizabeth Cobb prior to her marriage, confirmed Captain

Appleby's opinion. He wrote: '*I think that the cargo of alcohol, having been loaded in cold weather at New York early in November, and the vessel having crossed the Gulf Stream and being now in comparatively warm weather, there may have been some leakage, and gas may have accumulated in the hold. The Captain, having care for his wife and daughter, was probably unjustifiably alarmed and, fearing fire or an explosion, determined to take his people in the boat away from the vessel until the immediate danger should pass.*

'*Knowing what the duty of each man would be, it is comparatively easy to reconstruct the scene with the evidence which we have. The boat was launched on the port side. The Captain got his wife and daughter into the boat and left them in charge of Mr Richardson (the first mate) with one sailor in the boat, while their Captain went for their Chronometer, sextant, Nautical Almanac and the ship's papers. Mr Gilling (second mate) would be getting the peak halliard ready to use as a tow rope. Another sailor would be tending the painter (a length of rope made fast to the inner sides of the ship) and a fourth would be at the wheel. The cook gathered up what cooked food he had on hand.*

'*There is some evidence of haste in the act of leaving the vessel. The sailors left their pipes. The main staysail was not furled. The wheel was left loose. The binnacle was displaced and the compass broken . . . It may well have been that just at that time came an explosion which might have accounted for the fore hatch being upside down on deck as it was found.*

'*Whatever happened it is evident that the boat, with ten people in her, left the vessel and that the peak halliard was taken as a tow-line and as a means of bringing the boat back to the Mary Celeste in case no explosion or fire had destroyed the vessel. Probably a fresh northerly wind sprang up, filled the square sails, and the vessel gathered way quickly. The peak halliard, made fast at the usual*

*place on the gaff, would be brought at an acute angle
around a stanchion. With a heavy boat pulling at the end,
it is no wonder that the halliard parted.'*

Of all the theories, the possibility that the crew of *Mary
Celeste* panicked in fear of an explosion in the cargo of
alcohol, that they put away their boat on the end of the
main peak halliard, is the most convincing. In their
evidence in the enquiry before the Vice Admiralty Court,
those of the crew of the *Dei Gratia* who saw her witnessed
that her running rigging was in disarray. Deveau, the first
mate, testified that the main peak halliards were broken.
Seaman Lund, who accompanied him to Gibraltar, confirmed his evidence. Both said that there were no remains
of a painter or boat's rope fastened to the rails. It is
possible that it never occurred to them that the main peak
halliard which they found broken and which they subsequently repaired to get the ship into order to sail her to
Gibraltar, might be a key to the mystery.

It is also evident that the possibility of an explosion in
her cargo never occurred to Her Majesty's Attorney
General. Anyhow, it was not the sort of explanation he
wanted to believe. He had his own notions. In fairness, the
Americans, on their side, were not without prejudice.

A hundred years after, truth is as dark as Eleusis. I am
not even sure that anybody wants it otherwise. Perhaps
Captain Briggs, his family and his crew, didn't die in vain.
He left behind, for the rest of us, the fascinating problem
of what really did happen.

12. THE ENIGMA

To sum up, it is worth recapitulating the essential evidence.

Some extraordinary circumstance must have prevailed to explain how the Captain of *Mary Celeste* vanished with his wife and infant daughter, and seven crew, from a ship which was well-provisioned and in good order. She was in such sound shape that she sailed by herself, apparently for ten days, a distance of seven hundred and fifty miles on the course she was meant to take. It is no wonder that people have questioned what happened from that day to this.

It is proven, in spite of the legends, that she had a ship's boat, a yawl which would just about have supported nine adults and a child. But, at best, it would have been a shell in the Atlantic swell in midwinter. The stories of the unfinished breakfast, the cat in the cabin, the food warm in the galley, won't stand – unless the crew of the *Dei Gratia* were united in an unusual conspiracy. Certainly they had every opportunity, during the days that they were bringing the brig into Gibraltar, to remove incriminating evidence. As they had a ship's boat of their own it is conceivable, however improbable, that they tipped the yawl overboard to confuse the trail.

Dismissing the more fantastic solutions, the theories as to what actually happened may be resolved into four possibilities: (1) Mutiny (2) Conspiracy (a) A maniacal captain (4) An unusual natural phenomenon.

Mutiny was the immediate conclusion of Royal Naval Officers, called in by Mr Solly Flood. They took the view, with precedent to guide them, that it was the usual explanation of anything which destroyed good order in a ship. They were confirmed in their opinion when they learnt that *Mary Celeste* carried a cargo of alcohol. Given half a chance their experience was that seamen would drink anything. Their training, their whole code, required them to believe that no captain would desert his command except under duress. On the thinnest of evidence they declared that this was the only possible solution. The Captain of *Mary Celeste*, his family and officers, had been murdered by a drunken crew, and the mutineers had rowed off to make a landfall at St Mary's six miles away. They were convinced that it was the mutiny on the *Bounty* in reverse; the mutineers taking to the ship's boat after they had disposed of the Captain. It is essentially the theme which Laurence Keating exploited in his fiction *The Great Mary Celeste Hoax*.

As time passed by, and there was no news of mutineers, Mr Solly Flood concerned himself with the position in which the *Dei Gratia* said that the *Mary Celeste* was found. He determined that the *Dei Gratia's* story was unacceptable; that there was a darker explanation of what had occurred. He suspected a conspiracy between the two captains to get salvage money.

No abandoned ship, he decided could have sailed the distance that it was claimed she had sailed. By implication he pointed his fingers at the *Dei Gratia*. The last date in the log must have been altered. In his cross examination in court he made much of the fact that, from the time the crew of the British brig had taken her over, they had kept no log of their own movements. In the nature of their predicament, that was scarcely surprising; but it didn't deter Mr Flood. He was satisfied that no ship could set such a course with no helmsman at the wheel.

Yet it is a matter of history that the schooner *William L. White*, abandoned off Delaware Bay in 1888 during a blizzard, sailed for ten months and ten days, a distance of more than five thousand miles. She followed a course at an average of about thirty-two miles a day, indicating a speed of about one and one-third knots. With a few sails, and a favourable drift, it is not unbelievable that *Mary Celeste* might have compassed seven hundred and fifty miles in ten days.

Dr Oliver Cobb, who in his early years sailed before the mast gave his expert opinion to Charles Edey Fay: '*As the vessel sailed away after the change of wind which is reported to have come (and being headed easterly with a northerly wind), there were three sails drawing: foresail, lower topsail, and upper topsail. The foretopmast staysail and jib, being set on the port side, would not be of much use except as they would tend to prevent his vessel from coming into the wind and so keep her more steadily on her course. From 25 November to 5 December, northerly winds prevailed. The speed would be 3 to 4 miles per hour with ordinary winds, but the course sailed would be far from straight. She probably went easterly at about 2½ miles per hour, or, say 60 miles per 24 hours, for nearly eight days – or 480 miles. Then came a sudden change of wind – a squall perhaps. She came into the wind – shipped a sea (which accounted for the water in the galley and most of that in the hold, as the forehatch was off) – lost her foresail and upper topsail, and then filled away on the starboard tack ... The jib and foretopmast staysail were now set to draw, and the yards had worked round so that the lower topsail would draw on the starboard tack. She was now headed westerly. If she went westerly at 2 miles per hour, a total of 96 miles, the net distance covered would be 384 (470 less 96) miles, approximately the distance of 378½ between the probable point of abandonment and the point of actual discovery.*

Dr Cobb's computation leaves a few hundred miles to be accounted for, if the crew of the *Dei Gratia* read her position right. Anyhow, he is guessing what the weather might have been, and the behaviour of the ship with no one at the wheel. But it is evident that *Mary Celeste* was likely abandoned on the date and in the position that the log slate indicated that she was; and found in much the latitude and longitude where *Dei Gratia* reported that she sighted her.

The suspicion of a conspiracy between Captain Morehouse and Briggs is weakened. The only damned spot is the suggestion that they were portside friends. But it seems that Mr Solly Flood knew nothing of it. If he had he would surely have made a meal of the matter.

J. G. Lockhart, a responsible writer of sea stories, started the hare that Captain Briggs might have gone mad. He published his theory in his book *Mysteries of the Sea:* '*My solution was suggested to me by the horrible and authentic story of the Mary Russell, a brig sailing from Barbadoes to Cork in 1828, whose Captain went off his head and, with the assistance of two apprentices, first bound and then butchered the greater part of his crew, two men, both badly injured managing to escape from him and to hide in the hold. I suggested that the presence of the harmonium and of religious books and music in the cabin of the Mary Celeste might possibly be the clue to a similar tragedy; that the Captain, a man of excellent character, might have developed religious mania, and, with the strength and cunning of the homicidal lunatic, have attacked, overpowered and murdered his wife and child and crew, taking them one by one and unawares; and that finally, the mad Captain of an empty ship, he may have recovered his senses, as homicidal maniacs generally do, and, horrified by his crimes, have thrown himself overboard.*'

In a later book, *A Great Sea Mystery* (1927), Lockhart retracted. '*All this was merely conjecture, of which little more could be said than that, although there was not a lot of positive evidence in its support, it roughly accounted for most of the facts as I have given them.*'

Unfortunately he was not correct in some of his basic facts. He generously admitted in his later work, not altogether accurate either, that he had been misinformed. Yet, like mud, another theory stuck. It maybe, nobody knows for certain, that Captain Briggs did indeed go off his head. While it is an improbable explanation it is nevertheless unarguable that the conduct of people, especially people confined in small ships for long periods, is also unpredictable. Out of my own experience I am not sure that under pressure anybody remains completely sane. Yet in my own judgement, and the judgement of others, Lockhart's theory is not good enough.

The most remarkable detail is that Briggs, if his ship's company were all alive, left his vessel without as much as a note of explanation. He must have been in a helluva hurry. So, it appears, were his crew. The crew left behind their pipes, and their washing. The Captain only had time to collect the ship's chronometer, sextant, navigation book, and ship's register. On paper, Captain Briggs broke a tradition of the sea. He should have been the last to desert her.

And it was the last thing that you might have expected him to do. *'Benjamin Spooner Briggs was born at Wareham, Massachusetts, on 24 April, 1835. He was the second of the five sons born to Captain Nathan Briggs and his wife, Sophia Cobb. All of the sons but James were brought up by their father to follow the sea, and two of the four became master mariners at an early age.... Benjamin's father, Captain Nathan Briggs, appears from his letters and voluminous sea journals to have been poet and philosopher as well as practical and successful master mariner. Although kind and affectionate in all his family relationships, he was a strict disciplinarian aboard ship ... He was a Spartan father when it came to having his sons on shipboard. They had to do the regular work of sailors, take their trick at the wheel, stand watch, help reef and furl sails. The Captain expected his boy to be the first man aloft in an emergency....*

'In 1824, Captain Nathan Briggs made his first voyage across the ocean, as master of the schooner Betsy and Jane. When he shipped his crew, he wrote into the articles of agreement: "No grog will be allowed on board." Others

copied this and, in 1840, it became part of the standard form of agreement. This attitude towards liquor, both on land and sea, also became one of the fixed principles of his son Benjamin.'

No Captain in the record could have better recommendation. Benjamin Briggs was unusually qualified to command a ship; a ship, too, in which he had in his care his wife and daughter. In his thirties he was in the prime of his life. He had a useful share in the property that he was sailing. He might well have expected to retire to New England, with a reasonable pension, to join the son he had left behind.

It is interesting that he belonged to a seafaring family which had been cursed with ill-luck. His brother had been lost on shipboard, his sister in a shipwreck. Two other brothers died at sea of yellow fever. His father, Captain Nathan, survived the ocean to be killed by lightning as he stood at the doorway of his home. Benjamin is described by a member of his family as 'a man who spoke in a quiet tone of voice, and with an inclination to reticence'. It is said that he was very familiar with the Bible, which he read regularly. 'On occasion he "gave testimony" at prayer meetings. On his trips to Gibraltar he joined a Masonic Lodge.'

If he was all that, he was a very strange character to be commanding a trading brig; a man who, in deep religious devotion, would lose his nerve in a worldly emergency, whatever that emergency was. I find it hard to believe that he was just that sort of person. His descendants are properly anxious to defend him. My own guess is that he was not quite as holy as the New England version, or quite as wicked as the bogus accounts suggest. Briggs was somewhere, as we all are, between the two.

In worrying out the question it is worth telling that Mrs Frances Richardson, the widow of the first mate of the *Mary Celeste* – who died in 1937 at the age of ninety-one – remained convinced that her husband was the victim

* Charles Edey Fay.

of mutiny and murder. Oliver Deveau, the first mate of the *Dei Gratia*, died in 1912 in Nova Scotia. He was seventy-six. To the end of his days he insisted that the *Mary Celeste's* crew abandoned her because they thought she had more seawater in her than she had. Captain Deveau, as he subsequently became, seems to have been a simple fellow. Not in him to look for mystery. He left that for posterity to wrangle about.

Captain Morehouse, whose opinion as a first witness is clearly important, believed that on the morning of November 25, the *Mary Celeste* was becalmed a few miles to the north of the dangerous coast of Santa Maria in the Azores; that a current began to drive her towards the shore; and that the crew, in sudden panic, took to the boat. '*Probably they intended to stand by and, if a breeze sprang up, to rejoin the ship; but unfortunately they did not take the precaution of attaching the yawl by a line to the Mary Celeste. So, when the desired breeze came the brigantine careered away from them and, row as strongly as they could, they were unable to overhaul her. Captain Morehouse believed that ultimately the boat was driven ashore and beaten to pieces in the surf at the foot of the cliffs, while all those in her perished. This view was also taken by Captain James Briggs, a brother of the missing Captain.*'*

Captain J. H. Winchester, the principal owner of *Mary Celeste*, the same who gave evidence in the enquiry in the Vice Admiralty Court at Gibraltar, was himself convinced that Captain Briggs abandoned the *Mary Celeste* in the apprehension that the cargo of alcohol was on the point of exploding. He confided his conviction to his grandson, Mr Winchester Noyes.

'All in all, Dr Oliver Cobb's theory of a broken halliard offering the main clue to the solution of the mystery supports Captain Winchester's theory of a disturbance in the cargo of crude alcohol. The crew, in fear of an explosion in the hold, launched the brig's only boat on

* J. G. Lockhart.

a line attached to the main peak halliard. It is the least thrilling of the theories which have been advanced. It is also the only one, in the light of all the known evidence, which cannot be knocked down. That the main peak halliard was broken, and all the witnesses agreed that it was – they had to replace it – is an undoubted fact of the case. The halliard would not have been broken unless it had been employed for an unusual purpose.

The enigma remains that Captain Briggs, an experienced seaman, supposedly lost his nerve when there was an explosion in the barrels of alcohol in the hold. It is a sailor's superstition that a hatch thrown upside down is a sign of ill luck. In fact, if gas had collected in the hold, it was the healthiest thing that could have happened. It let in the fresh air.

It may be that if Briggs hadn't got a wife and infant daughter aboard he would have been less inclined to abandon his ship. Anyhow, it must have been in sheer panic that he lowered his wretched little yawl into the cruel Atlantic and chanced her, overloaded, to go God knows where. If the *Mary Celeste* had blown her timbers she would still have been a better bet for survival than the ship's boat. With all his experience of the sea, Briggs must surely have known that. Yet, if the most reasonable explanation is accepted, he behaved like a fool; worse, a frightened one.

Perhaps some of the fantasies which have been built about the *Mary Celeste* deserve greater credence. Captain Briggs commands no respect if he indeed abandoned his ship, with his wife and child, because there was a rumble in the hold. Captains are captains because they don't panic in an emergency. It would be nicer to believe in the story of the giant octopus whose tentacles took them off, one by one.

13. EPITAPH

'Date of Surrender, January 3, 1885; where surrendered, Mirageone, Haiti; cause of surrender, vessel lost by stranding January 3, 1885 on the reefs of the Rochelais, near Mirageone, Haiti; on board, none lost: – Maritime Register, 28 January, 1885.'

It is told that, even when *Mary Celeste* was released from the charge of the court in Gibraltar in 1873 there was trouble in enlisting a crew to take her to Genoa, and unload her cargo. Sailors, ever superstitious men, were reluctant to serve on a ship which they regarded as a hoodoo. It seems that she was haunted with fear for the rest of her career.

Between 1872 when she lost her crew and 1885, when she was lost herself, she changed hands seventeen times. 'She lay for more than a year in the Erie Basin, and no one wanted her. The broker who had her for sale reported that one day a negro or mulatto called on him and said he wanted to put his son in the African trade. He took him along to the vessel, crossed the ferry to Brooklyn, and just as they were leaving the ferry house on the Brooklyn side the negro said: "Say, Mister, what do you call this brig?" The broker said: *"Mary Celeste!"* and at these words the negro, who had seemed a man of some intelligence, was filled with terror, and shouted: "Go away from me, I won't have nothing to do with her." He broke away from the man, ran back, and jumped on the ferry boat as if panic stricken. The broker, amused that even a "nigger", as he called him, should baulk at the name, was more than ever convinced that she was an unlucky ship.'*

* From J. G. Lockhart reporting a correspondence with Frederick J. Shepard, of Buffalo, with reference to a ship owner named Raphael de Florez who said that he was ignorant of the details of the story but that he knew the ship.

I am doubtful whether the anecdote is acceptable. It echoes too clearly Conan Doyle's story of the coloured man with a holy respect for an idol. It supports my conviction that fiction writers invent what ultimately goes as truth. What is unquestionable is that for twelve years after she went into history none cared to know anything about *Mary Celeste*. She rotted on wharves where nobody wanted her. By that time she probably wasn't worth the saving. In the end she passed out in the most wretched circumstances that a ship can die.

She was bought for a song by a consortium 'of Boston' in 1884. She sailed with a cargo which was described as: *'475 bbls.alewives, 135 plgs.ale, 64 cases boots and shoes, 10 bbls bread, 4000 lbs. butter, 10 bbls. beef, 87 boxes codfish, 67 drums do., 30 coils cordage, 34 cases canned fish, 30 pygs. domestic, 50 pygs. furniture...'*

No need, in the fat and largely incomprehensible list of her cargo, to look further. The whole lot was bogus. In dead calm and clear weather, her last captain ordered the man at the wheel to run her aground on a coral reef. Presumably, he offered his crew a reward. Their lives were never in danger. Their Captain, Gilman C. Parker, was confident that they would all make a handsome profit. It was a sort of introduction for Captain Lucy's story of a ship stuffed with gold.

They were caught out. The underwriters, suspicious of a ship which was over insured, noticed that in the part of the cargo listed as ale, more bottles had been billed to a barrel than a barrel would hold. They asked Mr Kingman Putnam (a brother of the famous Major Putnam who founded the book publishing business) who was acting as surveyor in the loss of a schooner on the south coast of Haiti if he could take the second case in his stride.

'On arriving at Port-au-Prince Mr Putnam called on the firms to whom the merchandise carried by the *Mary Celeste* had been consigned, and was given copies of the letters they had received from the shippers at Boston. He then rode across on horseback to Mirageone, where the brigantine's crew had been landed after the wreck. There, he found that Captain Parker, the master, had sold the entire cargo, which had largely been salved, to the United States Consul, Mr Mitchel.'

Mr Mitchel was no Horatio Sprague. He bought the entire cargo of the ship, which had been insured for $30,000, for $500. No doubt he thought he was on to a good thing. But Captain Parker had sold him a pup. On inspection it was discovered that the bottles of ale were filled with water. A case which had been shipped as cutlery, and insured for $1,000, contained dog collars worth about $50. The cargo of boots and shoes were shoddy rubbers. It is interesting that Mr Putnam, in his enquiry, managed to obtain a consular invoice from Mr Mitchel certifying that the goods, such as they were, were from the last cargo of *Mary Celeste*.

Cases of the rotten stuff were shipped to a lawyer in Boston who indicted the master of the *Mary Celeste* on a charge of barratry and conspiracy, and the shippers with him. The case, like the first mystery, was never resolved.

'*Mr Putnam returned to Haiti as a Deputy-Marshal, armed with powers to subpoena witnesses and with an order for Mitchel to return with them to stand his trial. The subpoenas, though of doubtful value which lay, strictly speaking, beyond the jurisdiction of the United States, enabled Mr Putnam to extract the required documents from the merchants of Port-au-Prince. From there the steamer took Mr Putnam on to Mirageone where a Haitian general came on board with the news that the deliquent consul, Mr Mitchel, was about to take to the woods. However, he assured Mr Putnam that all would be well, for the President of the Black Republic, anxious to oblige, had instructed him to take a file of soldiers and put Mr Mitchel willy-nilly, aboard the steamer. But the steamer, the Saxon, sailed under the British flag. Mr Mitchel was an American citizen; and the Saxon, not being allowed to carry passengers, Mr Putnam appeared on the ship's list as "chaplain". The abduction from Haitian territory, of an American citizen by the chaplain of a British vessel might have raised all sorts of international complications; so the Haitian general's offer was reluctantly declined.'*

What happened to the runaway consul is not recorded. On March 29, 1885, it was reported in the newspapers that Captain Parker of Winthrop, Massachusetts had been arrested the day before by the United States Marshal, 'on a charge of having purposely wrecked his brig, the *Mary Celeste*, on a coral reef off Haiti.' The wilful wrecking of a vessel, defined as barratry, was an offense 'which was punishable by death under the United States laws'.

It was testified in court that 'it was a clear day and the sea was smooth: that the reef on which the vessel struck was plainly marked on the chart and clearly visible'; that 'the wheelman saw the reef, changed his course, and, on the Captain's orders, immediately set it back, with the result that the vessel went on the centre of the reef.'

Also said on oath was 'what was practically a dummy cargo of fish, rubber shoes, etc., was put on board and heavily insured'. The vessel, according to report, was insured for $25,000 and 'the arrest was made at the instance of the insurance companies on the testimony of the mate.'

The result of the trial in Boston was, surprisingly, that the jury disagreed. Mr Putnam is quoted as saying that 'they stood nine to three in our favour. The odd men out declined to convict Captain Parker on the charge of conspiracy for fear it might influence the jury who were going to try him for barratry....

'A notice for a new trial was immediately given. All the shippers came forward and acknowledged their guilt. One firm which had collected a loss of $5,000 on some rotten fish, paid it back with interest. It also paid $ to the government for the loss of the suit.'*

* My authority is Charles Edey Fay.

Mary Celeste

Captain Parker was never brought to trial on the capital offence. He died three months before the new trial which had been ordered could take place. Three months later the first mate on the *Mary Celeste*'s last voyage died, too. 'One of the guilty shippers committed suicide. All the firms concerned in the fraud failed and went out of business. The *Saxon* was wrecked with loss of life on her next voyage; and even the schooner *Mary E. Douglas*, in which Mr Putnam made his first voyage to Haiti, coming to grief a little later.'*

It is proper to add that wreck and disaster was the common fate of sailing ships, wooden things without power which were easy victims of the merciless sea. But, for twenty-four years, the little brig of Canadian timber defied the traditional enemy throughout the oceans of the world. The men who sailed her, lost her, arrested her and finally wrecked her, showed all the weaknesses which man is heir to. The mystery of *Mary Celeste* is us.

* J. G. Lockhart.

14. THE THINGS PEOPLE SAY

Over the years I have exchanged correspondence with many people who have become interested in the fate of the *Mary Celeste's* crew. Letters, not all of them addressed to me, have passed into my possession. Early in my own enquiry, when I had already reached the conclusion that there can be no final solution of the mystery, I became increasingly intrigued with the theories which have emerged, and the plain lies, in the convolutions of human minds.

None, in that connotation, is more fascinating than Laurence J. Keating who wrote *The Great Mary Celeste Hoax*. I have a letter about him from the late T. E. Elwell (4:10:57): *'I knew Laurence Keating well. He was, or is, – I have no knowledge of his death – a liar, a confirmed plagiarist, and quarelsome withal. Early in 1923, a friend of mine, named Robert Flaherty, who knew him brought him to see me. At that time I was writing an article on the Mary Celeste which appeared in Chambers' Journal on July 2, 1923. Keating had never heard of the mystery, and said the whole thing was a fairy tale. When my article appeared, he was eaten up with jealousy, and asked if I was going any further with it. I said "No", I have written all I mean to write on the subject.*

'I saw no more of Keating – didn't want to – but my friend, who lived near Keating, told me that he was engaged on some spoof about the mystery, and that my friend had been asked by Keating for ideas as to how to treat the thing. My friend told him that if he was determined on spoof, something could be done about a salvage wrangle between the skippers of the Mary Celeste and the

Dei Gratia . . . In June, 1926, my friend brought Keating along to tell me that he had resolved the mystery, and had found the one-time cook, a Mr John Pemberton.'

Mr T. E. Elwell didn't believe a word of it. 'I reached for my hat and said: "Where is he?" "O.K.", said Keating, "he died three days ago, and was buried yesterday." Captain Elwell added: "They always die before anyone can see them." ' Keating himself died on March 16, 1954. I have a letter from his sister, Mrs Margaret McDonald, telling me that *'he had been ill for a long time. He never discussed his book with me, so I can't tell you anything about it. I don't think that he bothered about anything. He was too sick. I had him with me and my family for nearly forty years, and lost a good pal.'*

Laurence J. Keating, before his death, shows himself. He wrote a number of letters to F. J. Lambert, an acquaintance he was clearly anxious to impress. I have extracted the essential information – written on June 9, 1947:

'The English book, Great Mary Celeste Hoax, appeared in 1929. It was an artless book written for artless men who live in Sailors' Homes and Ships, who know what it's talking about. Nevertheless, it was met with never-ending abuse in this country, in U.S.A., and in the Colonies, from people who don't know what they are talking about. . . . I assure you that nobody anywhere except Laurence Keating, has ever had an opportunity to "research" the Mary Celeste, because all the relevant documents are the sole property of Laurence Keating's principals.'

It is enough to add one of the poor chap's more hopeless comments: *'Mr Charles Edey Fay (Yank!!) What a Yank! It's not me, I assure you. I have not read Charles Edey. I do fancy really he is having a "go" at Commander A. B. Campbell for I did hear that A. B. got wind that an abusive "buke" was after him at the time of his temerity (1942). "Me Lud" dared give his views on the Mary Celeste in the Sunday Dispatch. I do not think Com.*

Campbell is upset through abusive "buke", although I guess he is flabbergasted. Naturally, I can't go into the sinister side of this polecatting here.'

There was much more to Laurence Keating's letters. They are not worth recording. A psychiatrist might be interested in the inventions, which the fellow seems to have believed out of his own imagination. He could say, in one of his letters that *'John Pemberton's artless story is the true story. The plans of the brig which you have are the real plans of the Mary Celeste.'*

Keating knew nothing of it. He was one of those strange men who believed what he wanted to believe. The Irishry in him may have guided him as it guided Mr Solly Flood. His claim, like Mr Flood's, can be dismissed with a certain contempt.

There exists a letter, in the *Journal of Commerce* of September 6, 1927, which is worth quoting. Discussing the latest *Mary Celeste* solution, that by J. G. Lockhart, that the danger of the alcohol cargo exploding suddenly drove the master and crew off the ship, Captain J. L. Vivian Millett, of *Cutty Sark* fame, and a member of the Port of London Authority, 'mildly described Mr Lockhart's discovery as "piffle".'

'It is an impossible solution,' he said to the *Journal of Commerce* representative. *'The shipmasters of those days knew very well what a cargo of alcohol meant. They naturally kept it ventilated, and that is why one of the hatches was kept upside down on the deck. Captain Briggs was certainly not the man to abandon his ship on account of some mild alcohol fumes exploding in the hold. He would expect them in warm weather, and he prepared for them.*

'When I was master of the steamer Pembridge, I remember a very lucky voyage from Saigon to Dunkirk. The cargo was rice. I have never seen such a spell of fine weather before. For over forty days the sea was smooth. I took hatches off with every change of wind, five of them,

and they remained off day and night for the whole voyage. The rice was well ventilated. It was stated to be the best rice cargo ever imported by Dunkirk, and I received a handsome bonus.

'In the light of long experience,' Captain Millett added, *'on that part of the ocean where the Mary Celeste was discovered in such unusual circumstances I hold my belief that the solution of the mystery is Riff pirates. Even when I was a third mate on a steamer covering the sea near that part of the African coast, twelve years after the Mary Celeste we were in mortal fear of Moorish pirates. Ships were constantly being lost as a result of their raids.'*

Captain Millett's opinion is not supported by the records. There is no evidence that pirates, from the African coast, interfered with shipping in the second half of the nineteenth century.

I have another letter, dated August 25, 1957, from Mr W. J. Chambers: *'The fate of the crew of Mary Celeste, although perhaps the most outstanding mystery of its kind, is by no means the only one. I expect you saw in the Evening News (August 22, 1957) the case of the Carol A. Deering. Before my scrap books were destroyed by a bomb during the war I could have produced other earlier cases. More recently, we have had the Joyita and (possibly) the Kobenhavn, of which it seems pretty certain that there was no crew on board when she was driven on Tristan de Cunha.'*

Mr W. W. Banham, I am not sure how his paper got into my files, is an example of how absurd explanations have come to be accepted as fact. I was tempted to eliminate much of what he wrote. But, in his illiterate way, he said what he believed with no notion, unlike Keating, of financial gain. It sees, from his knowledge of sail, that he was a seaman. In an analysis of the case, it is not unimportant to examine what simple people like him have thought into it. It is not irrelevant that he tells of wonders that many, ever since Conan Doyle, would still prefer to believe:

'*Fifeen years before the mystery of the Mary Celeste, a similar event had taken place, in the self same waters. A ship had been found, intact, but without any sign of Captain or crew. It remained an unsolved problem, only to come to light again, when the question of the Mary Celeste arose, What was there, down off the West Coast of Africa, in equatorial waters, that could have caused these two odd mysteries? It was the day of sail, of sturdy men and ships, relying on the whims of nature to see them through from one global point to another. Only on very rare occasions would a vessel be able to make her destination direct, blessed with a following wind, her sails billowing out to port and starboard, butterfly fashion. Usually it was a long beat, or reach, or a tack, that was necessary to make good "over the ground". It makes it all the more difficult to believe, that two ships of sail with an interval of 15 years between them, should have had the same thing happen to them, at the same spot, in the vast expanse of the Oceans. What had lured them to this area? Was it just coincidence, a combination of relative seas, similar trade winds or streams, and weather conditions? One hundred years ago is a long time. During that period, ships have passed from sail to steam, from coal to oil, on to atomic. During that passing century, lots of things could have happened and changed, without the knowledge of man. If we believe the old sea captains of those days, great monsters lived in the vasty depths of the oceans, together with lovely maidens with tails of fishes, mermaids they called them. Certainly monsters did exist, call them sea serpents or what you will. It was about this time that one of Her Majesty's warships sighted a denizen of the deep. Dozens of her ship's company came up on the upper and poop decks to see it, and men clambered up the standing rigging to obtain a better view of the fishy stranger. A notation was made in the warship's deck log, and in due*

course a report was made to the Admiralty. Surely all
these well disciplined men, could not be wrong? It is
possible and probable that during this last one hundred
years, that such inmates of the deeps have become extinct,
unknown, unseen, or even realized by man. There is no
doubt that they did exist, and could have accounted for
both incidents. It is perfectly feasible that one of these
creatures, seeking its food, lived in that sea area, and de-
voured the crew of these two ships. Old sea prints of sea
serpents are all much of a "sameness", a picture of a long
snaky body with a head similar to a cow or horse, and
giving an impression of speed in the water. Usually the
head and neck was shown well up, several feet in length,
clear of the sea, as it cleared its way along, furtively looking for something to eat. These were tropical monsters and
could never be confused with whales. We can therefore*

---

* In a sea of balderdash it is remarkable that this assertion is true. In October, 1848, *H.M.S. Daedalus* (Capt. McQuhae) reported to the Lords Commissioners of the Admiralty that in the previous August, his crew had sighted a monster. 'I have the honour to acquaint you that at 5 o'clock p.m., on the 6th August last, something very unusual was seen by Mr Sartoris, midshipman, rapidly approaching the ship from behind the beam. On attention being called to the object, it was discovered to be an enormous Serpent, with head and shoulders kept about four feet constantly above the surface of the sea; and as nearly as we could approximate, by comparing with the length of what our main topsail-yard would show in the water, there was, at the very least, sixty feet of the animal a fleur d'eau, no portion of which was, to our perception, used in propelling it through the water either by vertical or horizontal undulation. It passed rapidly, but so close under our lee quarters that, had it been a man of my acquaintance, I should have easily recognised his features with the naked eye. The diameter of the Serpent was about 15 or 16 inches behind the head, which was, without doubt, that of a snake; and it was never, during the 20 minutes that it continued in sight of our glasses, once below the surface of the waters – its colour a dark brown with yellowish-white about the throat, It had no fins, but something like the mane of a horse, or rather a bunch of seaweed, washed about its back. It was seen by the quartermaster, the boatswain's mate and the man at the wheel in addition to myself...' Capt. McQuhae's dispatch agreed very largely with reliable seamen's reports which had been accumulating ever since the 18th century. At different times over thirty warships had reported huge massive creatures, of extraordinary appearance. Sea serpents have also been constantly reported by liners. The latest one was in 1947 which said that it had run into a monster and killed it.

imagine one of these now believed extinct creatures, over-hauling a luckless sailing ship. It looms alongside and scares living daylights out of the crew, by its hideously shaped head and fang incrusted mouth. With sharp incisive darting movements, like the tongue of an anteater, it gobbles up first one and then another. Any difficulty of swallowing would be overcome by submerging the human victim into the sea and drowning it first. One or two may have survived the initial onslaught by being between decks, but no doubt it was only a matter of time, before the creature smelt them out. No blood, no mess, or if there was, it happened outboard. So there we have it. Two ships winkled clean, with no one to tell the truth, as to what really happened. All this is of course conjecture, and in the case of the Mary Celeste it collapses completely, if the rumoured statement that the Captain's chronometer has been found and that descendants are said to be alive. How has all this come about and how did the survivors get ashore with the chronometer, without a boat being lowered from the mother ship! No other vessel had reported picking up ship-wrecked crews; yet things happened suddenly, for breakfast was only half-eaten. How comes it that in such circumstances, the Captain can retrieve his valuable chronometer and take it with him, for years afterwards, it is traced and proved to be that belonging to the Mary Celeste. How could all this possibly come about! What was the motive? How could human beings be transferred from a sailing ship, two or three hundred miles from land without boats? The answer is that there must have been water-borne transport, for aircraft were non-existent in those days. Now let us try and probe out the mystery. These two ships, with an interval of 15 years, between them, lose their white crews, and nothing more is heard of them, until a hundred years later, when their alleged descendants are discovered, their stories being backed up by the production of the chrono-meter. Round about the middle of the last century, sailing

ships running up and down the west coast of African
Continent, called into ports, (or off shore loading spots),
the area becoming known as the white man's grave.
Malaria, Beri-beri, and Black water fever prevailed, with
death around the corner. Yet what attracted the white
man? What made him accept the risks? Obviously the
answer is, as it has always been, wealth. Along these
parasitic infected shores, was gold and precious stones in
abundance. So much so, that soon an area was named the
Gold Coast. It required the ability of the white man to
abstract this known wealth. To seek and to find. The
hard manual labour must be left to the black native, but
he must be directed and controlled, and only white men
could do it. We do not know how the original handful
of white settled in the Gold Coast. Probably a genuine
ship-wrecked crowd, who soon intermixed with the
natives, and made the discoveries of potential mineral
wealth. If they could only get this valuable stuff away,
they could be rich. In the meantime, they were fighting
and losing fight against the prevailing tropical fevers, their
numbers getting less and less. An occasional seaman would
perhaps desert his ship being lured on by the stories of the
"Shangri-La" ashore. These "get rich quick at all costs"
individual types were of no value, soon lapsed into the
easy way of life with the natives, and were really trouble
makers between white and black. Yet white leaders and
masters must be found. It is not unreasonable to suppose,
that they could be induced to transfer from ship to shore,
under promise of "part of the kitty". Failing which, they
could be "Shanghaied" much in the same way as crews of
some of our ships at that time were. Captain Briggs of the
Mary Celeste may have been approached by the leader
of the decreasing white fraternity and a true picture of the
state of affairs presented to him. It is more likely however,
that the Captain was given a lurid account of all that
could be his, if he complied with what was required of
him, and that was the surrender of his white crew. These

*men would more than make good, the depletions caused by
the interval of the last 15 years, upon the previous captured
ships' company. We do not know whether Captain Briggs
fell in with the idea or not. Neither do we know whether
he had approached his crew and sounded them in regard
to a stay upon the Gold Coast, with promise of being well
rewarded? It was usual for the Captain's of ships in those
days to take their wives to sea with them and Captain
Brigg's wife and child were aboard. To him the whole
affair could have been merely a change of scenery, with a
rosy fortune awaiting him, when his local period of use-
fulness was ended. So we are left in some doubt as to
whether the whole affair was entirely voluntary. The fact
remains that all the crew left their ship, and subsequently
landed somewhere, because there is the evidence of the
descendants of the men concerned. We can only draw a
mental picture of how it was done. A precedent had
already been established by the taking off of the crew of
the earlier ship. The fact that the vessel was not sunk, was
to create a "red herring", to divert the attention away
from the real object, the abduction of the white crew. So
here again, the episode could be repeated and Captain
Briggs and his men no doubt reacted to what was required
of them. It could be that they were drilled into leaving
things just as they were, knowing that the Mary Celeste
would ultimately be found. That was just what they
wanted. The Ship to be found, for then their relations left
behind, would cling to the idea that their men folk were
alive somewhere and would eventually return. It was an
indirect message of hope for those left at home and it
worked. So, briefly, Captain Briggs, his wife and child
and the crew, were transferred from their ship and reached
land somewhere in the neighbourhood of the Gold Coast.
To have done this by open boat seems out of the question.
Let us delve into the problem for a moment and weigh
up the probabilities of such a thing happening. Her own
boats were all accounted for and were in place and correct.*

So it seems a boat was sent across from another ship, or an additional boat was carried upon her upper deck, a boat large enough to carry a minimum of eight persons. In the latter case, it would have to be launched overboard, in the absence of davits? & derricks, by swaying a yardarm. Supposing that they did this and manned the boat? Who reset the yardarm and trimmed the sails? For when the Mary Celeste was found everything was in ship-shape order. Of course, it could have been done, for two men to have remained behind and squared things off, and before the ship sprung too quickly ahead under sail, dropped overboard into the boat being towed alongside, and then slipped the painter, or tow rope. All this however seems too far fetched, and if the men were not in the know, the carrying of an extra boat would have aroused the suspicions of the crew. It has been mentioned that a ship's company might have lowered a boat, the former belonging to the whites already living ashore, it being a previous arrangement settled with Captain Briggs? He may have planned for this change over to take place providing the weather was suitable to the occasion and their ship's position. The second vessel is hardly likely to have overhauled the Mary Celeste unless Captain Briggs had employed delaying tactics, such as luffing up and taking the way off his ship two or three times. Going alongside under full sail at sea, introduces an element of extreme danger, particularly in regard to a ship carrying square-sails, such as the Mary Celeste carried in her foremast. The rigging and yards extend well outboard of the beam, and the two ships would have locked together. They could of course luff up and spill the wind, haul away their braces and bring the yards, "fore and aft". If this was done, and they deserted the Mary Celeste who trimmed the yards and set the sails of the latter and steered her back on to a tack? Therefore, in all the circumstances known, and assumed, the mystery of the Mary Celeste boils to this:

'Captain Briggs was lured by the promise of wealth,

to hand over his white crew, with or without their consent. It is probable that he had previously collected a crew, who were willing to take part in the gamble. Knowing what was ahead, and to allay suspicion he took his wife and child along with him.

'He explained to the crew what he intended to do, in the way of "throwing off the scent", by telling them to leave everything ship shape; there was to be no sign of a prearranged clear out. On the other hand, if they were ignorant of his intentions what better time to allay suspicion could have been chosen, than that of the middle of a meal, breakfast! The overhauling ship hails them at dawn. They hove to and all hands on the Mary Celeste rush up on deck full of curiosity and excitement. A boat is seen approaching, and all thoughts of a half eaten breakfast are forgotten.

'Under some pretext or other, an invitation to go aboard, or under threat of impending disaster, they drop down into the boat now alongside. The Captain sees his wife and child safely overboard, followed by the crew. Perhaps the last seaman and himself quickly release the brails, haul away and secure the braces, setting her off to gather on a tack, and then drop down into the waiting boat, the Captain being the last to do so in accordance with maritime custom.

'Perhaps he had already decided to take his valuable chronometer with him or on the other hand, picked it up as a last subconscious action before leaving the ship. He may even have looked ahead to the day when he would sail away, loaded with riches, when once more his trusty old chronometer, would have been a valuable aid to getting him home.

'The most reasonable theory in relation to the crew and Mrs Briggs is that they know nothing about the transaction at all. That, as stated earlier, they left the ship hurriedly, willingly and probably thinking that they were coming back. Hence Mrs Briggs' jewellery,

*the child's clothing and the seamen's effects were left
just as they were, intact, and as later discovered by the
Dei Gratia, who found her. The question of insurance
does not arise. It is doubtful whether insurance was even
thought of in those days. If it was, the ship was not lost,
but her crew had merely disappeared.*

*'Today, along the Gold Coast, now opened up to
modern development, can possibly be seen evidence of
the original white man and maybe from the crew of the
Mary Celeste, for here and there are "throw backs",
albinos, the result of black and white unions of many
years ago.'*

It is good to end this story with a letter from Charles
Edey Fay. *'It is probable'* he wrote, *'that no other vessel
in maritime history has been the subject of so many books,
magazines and newspaper articles. Regrettably, much of
the writing has been inaccurate, and some of it has been
unfair. The legends have multiplied with the passing of
time ... Although my book was written fourteen years
ago* (his own letter is dated May, 1956) *hardly a month
passes without an inquiry of some kind about the case.
You may not know that the book was written without
benefit of royalties, which is traditional with publications
sponsored by the Peabody Museum. My rewards, although
intangible, have been most gratifying.'*

Born May 26, 1875, in New York City, Charles Edey
Fay became a senior executive of the Atlantic Mutual
Insurance Company, one of the five companies which
insured the hull and cargo of the *Mary Celeste*. His book
contains a documentation of the evidence which is invaluable. He died, at an advanced age, in 1957. I trust that
he would not have disagreed with what I have written
here.

Appendix 1. MR FLOOD'S
LAST WORD

No portrait or photograph, so far as I can trace, exists of Mr Solly Flood. I just have an impression of him as an explosive Irishman, rather overweight, with a tendency to gout, vivid in complexion as he was in speech. There is no question that the case of *Mary Celeste* became his lifelong obsession. In puzzling his character nothing is more revealing than a letter he wrote twelve years after the legal case had ended to the American Consul in Gibraltar, still Mr Horatio Sprague.

In a remarkable postscript, added forty-two days after he had composed his main letter, it is evident that, even then. he had hopes that Captain Briggs would turn up and, presumably, that he could charge him with his professional fees. The communication to Consul Sprague, made after his retirement as Attorney General, exposes his personality better than any photograph. Needless to say, his claim got him nowhere.

Gibraltar, 9th January, 1885
P.S. 20th February, 1885.

My Dear Mr Sprague:

I have the honour to recall to your attention an event in which you have felt no inconsiderable interest. In December 1872 it became my duty as H.M.'s Advocate General and Proctor for the Queen in Her Office of Admiralty to institute and conduct in the Vice Admiralty Court of Gibraltar against a vessel and cargo and effects on board, which had been found derelict and brought into the port of Gibraltar by the British Brigantine *Dei Gratia*. It was alleged and afterwards proved that the derelict vessel was, when found, perfectly seaworthy and to have sustained no damage whatever from the perils of the sea or any accident, or to have been in any danger whatever, and that her cargo was such that under no circumstances could she have foundered, but that she had been wantonly disfigured and damaged for the obvious but ill disguised purpose of making her appear to have been abandoned as unseaworthy. She was well found and well provisioned. The whole, or at least apparently the whole of the personal effects of the Master, even including his watch, purse, hat and trousers with braces attached, were found in his cabin. Effects of his two mates and crew, of which some were new and of very good quality, were also found on board. The after hatchway through which access was obtained to the provisions, and the fore-hatch through which access was obtained to stores and barrels of alcohol, one of which had been tampered with, were both found open and uncovered, the provisions immediately under the open after hatchway, and the stores immediately under the open forehatchway, were found perfectly dry; the deck house and after cabins were found artificially deluged with water. A few and inconsiderable marks of violence were found on deck, but as the evidence proved the crew to have been in possession of the vessel for sometime longer than the master, the chief mate, and, as I expect, the second mate, they had an ample opportunity to remove appearances of violence had there been any. The vessel turned out to be the American Brigantine *Marie* (sic) *Celeste* valued in her damaged state at Gibraltar at $5,700 for salvage purposes, and her cargo to have been alcohol only which was valued at Gibraltar at $36,943 for salvage purposes, shipped by Messrs. Ackermann & Co., American citizens in New York, for Genoa. The vessel was owned by Mr J. H. Winchester and other American Citizens. She had been commanded by Benjamin S. Briggs, a brave and experienced American Citizen, and also had on board when she sailed, his wife, the accomplished daughter of an American clergyman and their little girl aged two years. Albert G. Richardson, also a brave and experienced American Citizen, had been her first mate. Her complement (sic) had consisted of a second mate and five seamen, of whose nationality and antecedents nothing was then known, but the name of the second mate and the names of four of the five seamen indicated them to have been either Germans or Danes. She had no passengers except the Master's wife and child, and had no accommodation for any.

Under these circumstances, I felt it necessary to cause repeated and minute surveys to be held on the vessel and on her cargo and to be present during all of them, and to spare no exertions no pains and no trouble to discover the fate of all the ten persons who had left New York in the vessel and also, whether any, and if any, what, and by whom, any outrage or other serious crime beside that of disfiguring and casting away the vessel, had been committed on board her or after her abandonment. After a prolonged enquiry the vessel was delivered to Mr Winchester who had the largest interest in her, and had claimed her and made good his claim upon giving security for salvage and the expenses of the Queen, and the cargo was delivered to the representatives of Messrs. Ackermann & Co. who had claimed and made good their claim, upon giving security for salvage and the expenses of the Queen, but the effects of the Master, officers and crew not having been claimed, remained in the custody of the Marshal subject to the costs and expenses of the Queen and to abide such claims as might be preferred thereto and be established to the satisfaction of the Court, and in default as forefeited to the Queen. The Court having learnt from an affidavit of the Marshal sworn in the cause that you were willing to become custodian of the effects supposed to have belonged to the Master, Officers and crew for which neither he nor the Court had convenient accommodation, and to have the care of them on his behalf as Marshal without prejudice to the warrant under which he held them and subject to the jurisdiction of the Court, made an order permitting him to deliver, and you to have the care of them in the manner stated. The retention of these effects within the jurisdiction of the Court was a necessity, inasmuch as it was the duty of the Court to investigate and decide upon all claims which might be made thereto and condemn them as forfeited to the Queen, and to insure their delivery to the proper officer of Her Majesty's Revenue if unclaimed within a certain period. There was a further reason why it behoved the Court to be especially cautious to retain these effects within its own jurisdiction, namely, that in the event of any claim being made to them, an opportunity would be afforded to the Court of making a further and more rigid judicial inquiry into the fate of all persons known to have been in the vessel and especially whether any, and if any, what violence had, as there was too much reason to fear, being committed against any of them, and thus advance the administration of justice which could not possibly be effected elsewhere. The effects were accordingly delivered into your care and a receipt taken for them which was filed in the Registry. Shortly afterwards but before final judgement was given, namely on the 4th April, 1873 you favored me with the perusal of a letter which you had just received from a gentleman at Uetersum in the island of Fohr under date of the 24th of the previous month making inquiries respecting the condition and appearance of the vessel when found, which impressed me very strongly – I may almost say, convinced me, that it was dictated by or on behalf of some of the crew who had left the vessel conscious of having been guilty of a great crime and desirous to learn whether they could safely emerge from concealment. Feeling assured that if they were kept in total ignorance of the evidence given in the cause, the retention of their effects, within the jurisdiction of the Court, aided by silence would probably reveal the mystery on which the fate of all who had sailed in the vessel and the cause of her abandonment were involved, I immediately requested you to inform the parties that you were not at liberty to give any information whatever respecting the condition or appearance of the vessel, and that all inquiries relating thereto should be addressed to me. I added that so great was the necessity of caution, that the Judge refused to permit a certain paper to be opened for the present, even for the purpose of furnishing a copy to the Governor who had officially requested a copy.

Under these circumstances, I decided to postpone making a demand for remuneration for my services. There is no salary attached to the office of H.M.'s Advocate General and Proctor or other emolument in suit(s) relating to derelict vessels except such as is customarily paid by the owners of the vessel, and of the cargo and other property found on board, for the recovery of which he has a lien which he may detain upon the vessel and upon cargo and upon all other property found in her if he has any fear that the owners or their bail are untrustworthy, but having had personal experience of the high honor, liberality and trustworthiness of the Citizens of the United States, I had no such fears either of the owners who had appeared or of their bail and having in view that the suit so far as it related to the effects of the Master, Officers and crew had not yet terminated and that the retention of those effects within our jurisdiction might lead to and assist further inquiry by the Court into their fate, and being desirous to expedite the payment of the fees then due to the Judge and the Registrar and of the Marshal's disbursements, I wrote to the Counsel who represented the owners of the vessel and their bail, and the counsel who represented the owners (of the cargo) and their bail, the letters of which I enclose a copy. Neither of those letters has ever been yet answered or even acknowledged by either of the gentlemen to whom they were addressed, or by their clients or otherwise; it cannot therefore be denied that those letters were, and ever have been understood by them, not as an abandonment or offer of an abandonment of my right to remuneration by them, but merely as an offer of an intention on my part to waive my lien upon the vessel and cargo and place my right to remuneration by them on the footing of a debt of honor, for it is inconceivable that if my letters were understood as conveying an abandonment of my right to remuneration, any Gentleman should condescend to accept even an offer of that nature or, above all, to treat it as unworthy of acknowledgement.

I refrained for some years from making any representation with reference to my remuneration, under the firm conviction that a proper time to make it would be when the retention of the effects and silence had elicited claims to those effects and renewed enquiry by the Court into the fate of the Master, Officers and crew, or when all hope that the effects would be claimed had imposed upon Her Majesty's Advocate General and Proctor the duty of applying to the Court to condemn the effects subject to my lien, to the use of her Majesty. The necessity for performing that duty had not arisen when in January last year, a Statement appeared in the

Cornhill Magazine professing to have been written by an eye-witness, and to describe the master* of the Captain of the *Marie* (sic) *Celeste*, his wife and child, and the death of all the crew. This was followed up by the insertion in a newspaper published at Kropp, a small village in Holstein, of false statement(s), the obvious object of which was to stifle inquiry into the fate of the Master, Officers and crew of the *Marie* (sic) *Celeste*. I, and the German and Danish Consuls at my request, entered into a correspondence with various persons, which is not yet completed, but which, as far as it has proceeded, has tended to confirm my belief that the letter which, in April 1873 you sent to me for my perusal was dictated by survivors of the crew of the *Marie* (sic) *Celeste*. In the meantime, I have learnt from you that the effects upon the retention of which, in Gibraltar, I had for so many years been relying, for a solution of the mystery, had unfortunately been removed from the Jurisdiction of the Courts of Gibraltar, in January 1874, and consequently that the prosecution of a Judicial Inquiry into the fate of the missing persons, in which I might have assisted, had become impossible, and I should then have felt it no longer necessary to forbear from making a representation of my claim to remuneration, but that an inquiry by means of correspondence was then in progress. That correspondence has been protracted and is still being continued, but as it may last for some time longer, I think further postponement of my claim unnecessary. While abstaining from considering from a legal point of view the non-acceptance of the proposal contained in my letters of the 18th April, 1873, I desire to express my unabated confidence in the honor, liberality and trustworthiness of all the American people, and that in response to this communication, means will not be found wanting to requite my arduous labors and zeal not merely for the protection of the rights of individuals, but for the advance of public justice in which the whole American people are interested.

I further transmit for your perusal a fair copy of my minutes of such of the proceedings in the cause as I took

* The word 'murder' appears to have been inserted here by Consul Sprague in the belief, no doubt, that murder was what Mr Flood intended to say but wrote 'master' instead.

part in, down to the 18th April 1873, but these dry minutes exhibit to a very limited extent my efforts for the attainment of justice, and my special sympathy with the families of the Captain and his wife, and the Chief Mate and his wife.

I have the honour to be, my dear Mr Sprague,
    Yours most truly,
        (signed) Fred'k. Solly Flood.
        Her Majesty's Counsel and lately Her Attorney General and also Her Advocate and Proctor.

P.S. 20th February 1885.

I delayed transmitting this letter as I had no sooner written it than I was led to expect further information respecting the missing persons who had been in the *Marie* (sic) *Celeste*. I have now received some information, but it is so imperfect as to render further inquiries (word missing). However, I now transmit this letter as I think it contains all that is necessary for the present purpose.

(Signed) Fred'k. Solly Flood.

In the Cathedral of the Holy Trinity in Gibraltar, there is a brass plate commemorating Mr Flood:
'Sacred to the Memory of Frederick Solly Flood of
Slaney Lodge, County Wexford, Ireland, Esqr.,
Eleven years Attorney General of Gilbraltar.
Born at No. 8 York Place, London 7 August 1801.
Died at Gibraltar 13 May, 1888.'
The plate also shows a coat of arms with the motto 'Vis Unita Fortior', several texts and a statement that it was erected by Mr Flood's sons and daughters.

Appendix 2. THE SHIP

No contemporary painting or photograph was made of *Mary Celeste*. An unsigned painting, when she was singledecked and named *Amazon*, was made at Marseilles in November, 1861. It is now exhibited at Aulac, New Brunswick. But it is no guide to her subsequent appearance.

How she looked when she was discovered as a derelict has hitherto only been recorded in a crude woodcut. John Worsley's water colour in this book is the first by a marine artist to reconstruct her as the crew of the *Dei Gratia* saw her through the glass.

Although *Mary Celeste* is a popular subject of ship-modelling kits, it is remarkable how inaccurate most of them are. In fact, every detail of her is known. The diagrams which follow show the layout of the upper and lower decks:

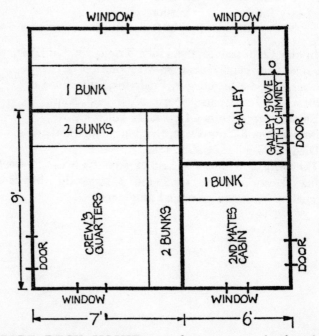

FORE DECK HOUSE: 13 feet square: six feet in height above deck. Made of thin planking, painted white. There is a sill, 6 to 9 inches at base of sliding doors

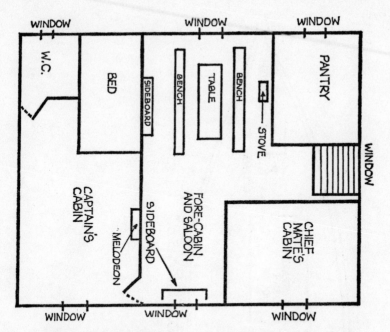

MAIN DECK HOUSE: 14 feet wide by 18 feet long (approx.). Made of thin planking, painted white. A skylight with six panes of glass on each side illuminates the forecabin and captain's cabin. Entrance into cabin is by hatch and sliding door down companionway on the forrard end of ship

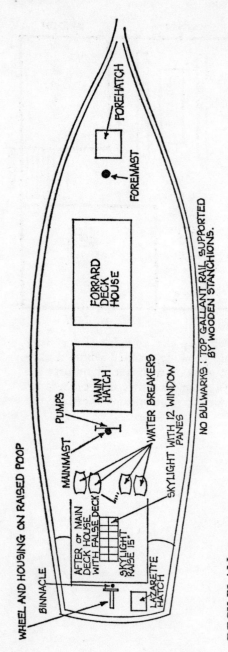

WHEEL AND HOUSING ON RAISED POOP

BINNACLE

AFTER or MAIN
DECK HOUSE
WITH FALSE DECK

SKYLIGHT
RAISE 15"

LAZARETTE
HATCH

MAINMAST

PUMPS

WATER BREAKERS

SKYLIGHT WITH 12 WINDOW
PANES

MAIN
HATCH

FORRARD
DECK
HOUSE

FOREMAST

FOREHATCH

NO BULWARKS : TOP GALLANT RAIL SUPPORTED
BY WOODEN STANCHIONS.

DECK PLAN
Length: 103 feet
Breadth: 25·7 feet
Depth: 16.2 feet
Cabin Height: 6 feet to 6.8 feet
Capacity under tonnage deck: 271 : 79
Deckhouse: 2 feet approx. above main deck

Appendix 3. THE CREW'S EFFECTS

The list of the property left aboard by the crew of *Mary Celeste* is essentially unimportant, but ineffably sad. The inventory, made by the Marshal of the Vice Admiralty Court, says so much about the sort of things that we all treasure which, in cold print, are so pathetic.

Chest No. 1 containing: a carpet bag; a pair of slippers; a hat; a bag; two vests; three pairs of drawers; a pair of trousers; three woollen shirts; four cotton shirts; a comforter; six pairs of cotton socks; a pocket book; two pairs of braces; a coat.

Chest No. 2 containing: eight books; a slate; an octant; a cap; two pairs of pants; two undershirts; three white shirts; a coloured outside shirt; a coat.

Chest No. 3 containing: two coloured shirts; two white shirts; three pairs of pants; an undershirt; two jackets; a package of letters; a vest; a hat; a cap; two comforters; three pocket books.

Chest No. 4 containing: a pair of shoes; a jumper; four vests; two caps; three white shirts; a pair of pants; a jacket; two pairs of stockings; a pair of mittens; a comforter; two flannel shirts; two outside coloured shirts; two pairs of drawers; two white flannel undershirts.

A canvas bag containing pieces of old clothing and bagging.

A canvas bag containing: two pairs of boots; old shoes; a doll.

An harmoniphon.

A child's arm chair.

A bag containing pieces of flannel.

Two lady's hats; one man's hat.

One valise marked D containing: six vests; three linen coats; six pairs of pants.

A canvas bag containing: two sheets; six shirts; one pair of drawers; two towels; three coats; two child's shirts; a pair of child's stockings; a night shirt; two pillow cases.

A trunk marked A containing: a mosquito net; two parcels of prints; four parcels of patterns; a small iron stand; a panama hat; a doll; a tool for cutting glass; four pairs of cuffs; two small metal boxes; two handkerchief; two neckties; a pair of braces; an envelope containing two freemason's documents; three scarfs; a set of draftsmen; two pairs of drawers; three pairs of pants; two shirts; a child's hood; three waistcoats; three woollen shirts; a pocket book containing $1 in Spanish Gold coin, $1 in American Silver coins, 25 cents in American coppers, together $2.25 cents; a small piece of net; a pair of cloth pants with suspenders; a crinoline; three dresses; two shawls; three coats; three books; a cartoon (sic) of ribbons &c., a piece of cloth; eighteen cloths; two night dresses; a pair of mittens; an old shirt; seven pairs of drawers; two towels (sic); five pairs of socks; a piece of cotton cloth; one cap; a piece of flannel; a silver watch; three child's pants; a pair of gloves; two pieces of cotton cloth; two pairs of child's shoes; two music books; a fan; two lady's breast pins; a small chain.

A sword; a log book; a sewing machine; a silk umbrella; a table cloth.

A trunk marked B containing: two lady's overcoats; a basket of needles, &c.; a cartoon (sic) of paper envelopes; three shirt bosoms; two pairs of cuffs; a piece of flannel; two dress bodies; three napkin rings; a box of seidlitz; a cartoon (sic) of paper collars; nine books; a parcel of letters; a package of starch; a parasol; two cloths; a bag of shells; two pieces of cotton cloth; a geometry box; a box containing razor, comb and brushes; a box of child's toys; two pairs of cotton stockings; a pair of mittens; a pair of india rubber shoes; a memorandum book; a comforter; a pair of socks; an opera glass case; six shirts; two skirts; four waistcoats; two woollen shirts; a pair stockings; three pairs of pants; a pair of drawers; a piece of a dress; a pair gloves; a scale; two parcel of flannels.

A canvas bag marked GWG containing: eight pairs of socks;

three undershirts; three handkerchiefs; a child's undershirt; two pairs of cuffs; three collars; two child's shirts; a napkin; a towel (sic); a child's dress; a cotton dress; a child's tie; a child's coat; a shawl; a vest; two pillowcases; three pairs of drawers; two pairs of woman's pants; four lady's shirts; a small blanket; a piece of a counterpane; a child's petticoat; two morning dresses; three night shirts; three sheets; three shirts; an undershirt.

A chest marked 'Arian Martens' containing: four shirts; four pairs of pants; five waistcoats; a morning coat; a woollen shirt; a piece of cloth; two hats; an overcoat; a pair of half-boots; a brush; a cigar case with three studs; six shirt collars; a belt; a cotton cap; a bag containing pieces of cloth; a tin canister containing a German document; a parcel of pieces of cloth; a sextant; a light coat; a razor strop; pieces of flannel; a lamp; a parcel of flax-seed; a straw fan; thirteen books; a paper book; a parcel of papers; a flute.

A trunk marked C containing: fourteen shirts, five pairs of drawers; three vests; six pairs of pants; three towels; ten books; a looking-glass; two pillow-cases; three coats; an undershirt; three pairs of cotton stockings; two albums; a cartoon (sic) of paper collars; a hair brush; two boxes containing letters & envelopes; four caps; a pair of slippers; a pair of shoes; a pair of half-boots; nine pairs of socks; a testament; a package of needles and thread; a linen coat; two mittens; a comforter; a gimblet, brush, soap, pins, razor &c.

Gibraltar 6th March 1873
     (Signed) G. W. Blatchford, Wrentham, Mass.
     (Signed) Horatio J. Sprague, U.S. Consul, Gibraltar.

'Inventory of the contents of a desk found on board the American Brig *Mary Celeste* of New York, by the Marshal of the Vice Admiralty Court of Gibraltar, and delivered to me this day, by the said Marshal; the said desk is supposed to belong to Captain B. S. Briggs, the missing Master.'*

* This inventory accompanied Consul Sprague's letter No. 138 dated 21 March 1873.

A desk containing: Twenty-one letters; an account book; a pocket-book; a ruler; two pieces of sealing wax; four United States postal stamps; a pencil; a paper cover containing sundry papers, envelopes and accounts; wafers; a case of leads; three receipts signed by J. H. Winchester & Co., New York, viz: for $1,500 dated 3rd October 1872; for $500 dated 16th October 1872; for $1,600 dated 22nd October 1872.

ACKNOWLEDGEMENTS

I have based the facts primarily on the transcript of the proceedings in the Vice Admiralty Court at Gibraltar in 1872–1873. For the Americana, I am indebted to Charles Edey Fay whose documentation of the case in his book *Mary Celeste* (1942) published in a limited edition by the Peabody Museum, Salem, Massachusetts, is invaluable. So, too, has been the late Mr T. E. Elwell's scrapbook.

I am obliged to Messrs. John Murray, the proprietors of the *Cornhill Magazine*. for permission to make a precis here of Arthur Conan Doyle's 'J. Habakuk Jephson's Statement' which first appeared in that journal. I owe much to Mr. Alan Wykes, the distinguished author who, in my early researches, helped me so much on my way. Mr. John Worsley, the marine artist, has painted what I believe to be the only authentic reconstruction of how *Mary Celeste* must have looked when she was first sighted by the *Dei Gratia*. The watercolour is now the property of Rear Admiral Godfrey place, vc dsc himself immortal as the Royal Naval officer who in 1943 in a two-man submarine mined the *Tirpitz* in a Norwegian fiord. The Parker Galleries kindly provided me with the print of the Rock of Gibraltar engraved in the middle of the nineteenth century.

I have referred to:
A Great Sea Mystery by J. G. Lockhart (1927)
Sea Fights and Shipwrecks by Hanson W. Baldwin (1956)
The Life of Sir Arthur Conan Doyle by John Dickon Carr (1949)
I also owe recognition to the impostors:
The Great Mary Celeste Hoax by Laurence J. Keating. (1929)
'*Abel Fosdyk's Story*' (*Strand Magazine*, November, 1943)
'*Captain Lucy's Story*' (*Daily Express*, September 24, 1924)
The photographs of the people most closely involved in the case are reproduced by permission of the Peabody

Museum, and with the co-operation of Mr Patrick Murray and the Edinburgh Central Library. I am grateful to Portia Holland who typed the manuscript, and Jennie Dereham for the index.

INDEX